KU-215-073

Miracles Today

Also by Edwina Allison:

With Barbara Gaskin:
A Love Lost – Life after the death of your partner
(Harvestime)

With Chris Youngman:
Holiday in Hell – A harrowing journey through M.E.
(Harvestime)

With Jo-Anne Cohrs:
Stigma – An AIDS widow's story
(Harvestime)

Miracles Today

Real-life stories of God's healing power

Edwina Allison

Harvestime

Published in the United Kingdom by:
Harvestime Publishing Ltd, 69 Main Street
Markfield, Leicester LE6 0UT

Copyright © 1991 Edwina Allison & Peter Reynolds
First published by Harvestime
First printed April 1991

All rights reserved.
No part of this publication may be reproduced or
transmitted, in any form or by any means, electronic or
mechanical, including photocopy, recording or any
information storage and retrieval system, without
permission in writing from the publisher.

British Library Cataloguing in Publication Data

Allison, Edwina
    Miracles today.
    1. Christianity. Healing
    I. Title
    248.29

    ISBN 0-947714-96-0

Typeset in the United Kingdom by:
Fine Line Publishing Services, Witney OX8 5SG
Printed and bound in the United Kingdom by:
Richard Clay Ltd, Bungay, Suffolk

Contents

Foreword

If there were any doubt that divine healing exists, *Miracles Today* has wiped it away for ever.

This book contains true stories of healing miracles. The testimony of ordinary men and women to Christ's healing provides all the proof needed that Jesus Christ, the Son of God, is still healing *today*.

During his ministry on earth, Jesus showed that he had power over nature, sickness, health and – ultimately – death itself. His miraculous acts are proof of his claim to be the Son of God.

Faith in him now – *today* – will enable you to claim a miracle, *if it is his will to grant it*.

These men and women – and there are millions more like them – are fortunate enough to have been granted the miracle of healing for his glory. Their testimonies are living proof of his divine grace and presence with us.

So throw away all doubt, and believe. Claim your miracle and trust in him.

David Suchet

To my husband Martin

With much love and many thanks for all your
encouragement

1

'At last I can outrun
my kids'

Peter Reynolds, Bath

I can well remember the first time I experienced the excruciating pain that was to become a part of my life for many years.

I was playing rugby. A fit, keen thirteen-year-old, all I cared about as I battled for possession of the ball was the excitement of the match. The fact that the second-row forwards behind me were huge strapping eighteen-year-olds didn't bother me at all.

Head down, legs braced, I positioned myself as 'hooker' in the front row of the scrum, ready to fight with the roughest of them to get my feet on that precious rugby ball.

Suddenly, the weight of the bigger players bore down on me. Unexpected pain ripped through my back.

Pain became an everyday part of my life. Doctors, tracing the beginning of my difficulties to the rugby match, understandably assumed that my back had been injured in the scrum. At that time no-one realised that I was manifesting the early, ominous symptoms of an incurable disease.

I started my first job when I was eighteen, working as a trainee accountant for the famous wine merchants, Harvey's of Bristol.

The pain in my back and legs often meant that I sat frozen for ten minutes, willing myself to stand up, dreading the agony that movement would bring. While others my age strode energetically down the street, I moved slowly, stiffly, sometimes with the small, measured steps of a ninety-year-old.

A Bristol orthopaedic consultant examined my X-rays carefully. 'You have a torn cartilage between your vertebrae,' he explained. 'Fluid is seeping out and putting pressure on your spinal cord and sciatic nerve, which runs down the back of your leg.'

'Will it ever get better?' I asked hopefully.

'Cartilage doesn't heal,' he said seriously. 'The only thing I can suggest is an operation to remove the damaged disc and cartilage and then to perform a bone graft. It may help you, but I can't guarantee it'll be successful. And if it isn't, you could be worse off than you are now.'

What a choice for a young man to have to make! I questioned the consultant further and discovered that I'd have to stay in bed for six months. With six months' convalescence I would be off work for a whole year!

My parents, wanting a second opinion, sent me to a Harley Street specialist. I also went to be examined by a well-known specialist at St Thomas's Hospital in London. But he only confirmed the bleak diagnosis of the local man. With no definite guarantee that I'd be any better off, I decided not to risk the operation.

I hated the restrictions placed on me by my condition. I was young and I wanted a good time. Every night I went out smoking and drinking in the pubs, trying to be one of the lads.

Outwardly I had a good time but inside I felt so empty. Surely there was more to life than this? When, at an evangelistic camp, I heard the good news that Jesus loved me, I immediately responded to the appeal for those who wanted to receive Christ.

'Now, Peter, you need to join a local church straightaway,' the counsellor advised me. 'And you must read your Bible and pray every day.'

I did everything he suggested. But the smoking and drinking continued and still the emptiness deep inside went unfulfilled.

A year later, when another evangelistic meeting was held, I responded again to the preacher's appeal. Up went my hand and down I went to the front of the meeting, praying a second time for salvation. I didn't know what I was looking for; I only knew I hadn't found it!

My double life was endlessly frustrating. I hated the inconsistency, the lack of purpose and the misery of being in pain. In a desperate attempt to find God I took a week's holiday and went to the Lake District to spend some time alone.

Two men were booked into the farmhouse where I was staying. One was a Methodist minister. The other, his brother, was a full-time worker with Youth for Christ. They were spending the week at the Keswick Convention, an annual Christian event.

As we talked, I shared my frustration. 'I want to change my way of living,' I confessed, 'but somehow I just can't.'

With their encouragement I went to the convention and for the third time I asked Jesus to come into my life.

Before they left, John invited me to a Youth for Christ conference, to be held in the autumn. And it was there that I heard that I needed to be born again.

Suddenly, I understood what had been missing. Every other time I'd prayed, I'd accepted salvation as an extra part of my life, a new dimension. But nothing else changed. I'd continued to live exactly as before, with church attendance, praying and Bible reading added on.

When I realised that I could be born again, that Jesus actually wanted to come inside and change me, tears of relief poured down my face. I gave him everything that made up me. My finances, my career, my dreams for marriage and family, the sort of house I wanted to live in, in fact, my entire future.

It was a new beginning. Smoking and pub-crawling were discarded without even a second thought. At last I had a purpose in life. I'd found a real relationship with God and I just wanted to serve him.

Accountancy didn't appeal to me anymore. I wanted to work with people, not money, so I applied to Bath University to do a degree in sociology. And there, at the Christian Union, I met Barbie, the loveliest girl I have ever met. She had golden hair and an Afghan coat!

The following year we went out to Afghanistan, where her parents lived, and we were married.

We returned to Bath after our honeymoon and settled there. A small church, started during our student days, was growing rapidly, and we were thrust into a leadership role.

As the years went by, the small church grew and I was appointed full-time pastor. It was fulfilling work, exciting, too, as together we discovered that God's power is real today. Miracles happened just as they had done in Bible days.

But despite our joy at seeing the people we prayed for being healed, at the back of my mind lurked a question. 'Why not me, Lord?' I wondered. 'I teach others that you're a God who heals, then limp off home.'

I had no doubt at all that God could heal me. I'd seen his power displayed countless times. Yet despite our prayers the pain in my back and legs was as bad as ever.

The crunch finally came when Barbie and I took our five children for a month's holiday to India. We so looked forward to showing them the places Barbie had known as a child. But while we were out there I contracted a bad dose of dysentery and became very ill.

I arrived home suffering from internal bleeding. My left ankle and right knee joint became so swollen I couldn't even get a pair of trousers on.

I dropped twenty-eight pounds in weight, and our doctor had me admitted to the Royal United Hospital. I was nursed in isolation until they were sure I hadn't brought home some obscure Eastern bug with me.

When Bryn Jones, leader of our team of church pastors, came to visit me, I looked and felt absolutely dreadful.

'Peter, I've started a fast for you today,' he said. 'And I'm not going to break it until you're well again.'

'Oh, don't, Bryn,' I groaned, touched by his commitment but alarmed at the possible consequences. 'I don't want *you* to die as well!'

It was a great relief when, at the end of the week, I began to improve. Bryn could break his fast.

Two years went by. Slowly I grew stronger, yet something wasn't right. My spine had begun to curve and I developed a permanent stoop. Then the internal bleeding returned.

I kept quiet about it at first, hoping it would clear up on its own. I felt reluctant to start again on the merry-go-round of hospital appointments and treatments.

After seven months I shared the problem with other pastors. They anointed me with oil and prayed fervently for my healing, but nothing happened.

It was so frustrating. A feeling of shame crept over me, as if I'd let everyone down by not responding to their prayers. I knew that living in health was part of God's covenant of blessing. And I wanted to live in the good of what I knew was mine by right as a

Christian.

Eventually, when it was clear that I wasn't getting any better, everyone ganged up on me and insisted that I went to see our doctor, who sent me along to the specialist at the hospital.

His diagnosis was conclusive. 'You have a condition called ulcerative colitis,' he informed me. 'The lining of your intestines is inflamed and ulcerated.'

I listened as he went on to explain more.

'This condition is incurable, I'm afraid,' he told me. 'You're going to have to accept the need for regular hospital visits for the rest of your life. Drugs will help you to manage the condition, but we can never cure you.'

I left his office pondering the implications of what I'd just heard. My next appointment was at the Hospital for Rheumatic Diseases. The specialist there investigated the curvature in my spine. His diagnosis was equally gloomy.

'You've got ankylosing spondylitis,' he told me. 'It often goes with ulcerative colitis. It, too, is an incurable disease. You've had pain since you were thirteen, I see.'

'But that was caused by an injury when I was playing rugby,' I pointed out.

He shook his head. 'Ankylosing spondylitis is a congenital disease,' he said. 'Not everyone actually develops it. Only a small section of the population have that particular tissue type. But the weakness was already there in you. It was that that brought about the pain you felt during the match.'

I left his office with more drugs and a regular appointment to be assessed and measured for further signs of curvature and deformity.

In the months that followed I cried out to God over and over again. As time went by and my illness continued, I began to question whether or not God actually wanted me to get well.

'Have I finished my usefulness?' I wondered. 'Is it time for the end of my life?'

The church was functioning well. We had a strong leadership now and I was sure they could manage without me.

My children were growing up. They and Barbie were used to managing alone when I went on ministry trips. They could cope if they had to.

Sitting in my office I wept. As a pastor I couldn't live a lie. I wasn't prepared to live the sort of life the doctors had spread out before me. God's promise was that I should be *healthy*. I couldn't settle for anything less.

Suddenly, there was a light tap on the door and, before I could pull myself together, it opened. Paul, one of the church elders, came in. He didn't need to ask what was wrong. One look at my face and he knew.

'Peter, you're going to be well again,' he declared firmly. 'You're going to be fitter than you've ever been before. Stronger and healthier, too.'

His words were more than just platitudes to comfort a sick man. They were life to me. Even as he spoke them I could feel my faith returning. Bit by bit I dared to believe once more that God would heal me.

During the next few weeks I held on to those words when discouragement threatened to engulf. Barbie's unwavering conviction, too, that I would be well helped to endorse a growing awareness that God would heal me.

Day by day the conviction grew within me that if God was going to heal me I should stop taking the drugs I'd been prescribed. It was a big decision, and not one to take lightly.

I was on steroids, sulpha drugs and anti-inflammatory drugs to ease the pain. I knew that simply to stop taking them without medical supervision would be very foolish. I also knew that it wouldn't be easy to convince the doctors that I was making the right decision in coming off them.

Because the consequences of such an action could be so drastic, I sat down with Barbie and the children and explained how I felt and what I was planning to do. They were one hundred per cent behind me, despite fully understanding the risks.

On my next regular appointment at the hospital I broke the news to the young lady doctor who was examining me. 'I can't live like this,' I said. 'I want to come off the drugs.'

The doctor was horrified. As patiently as if I were a three-year-old she went through all the reasons why I couldn't possibly stop taking them.

'You may have short periods of remission when you feel better,' she said. 'But even then you must continue to take the drugs. Otherwise, if the bleeding flares up again, it may be so severe that we can't control it and you could die.'

I remained politely adamant. 'I'm a Christian,' I explained. 'I believe that God's going to heal me.'

The doctor raised her eyebrows. 'I, too, am a Christian, Mr Reynolds,' she declared. 'And you don't get healed of this!'

'I'd like to be off all drugs within a month,' I said.

Seeing that I was determined, she reluctantly agreed but wrote on my medical records that this was against medical advice and entirely at my own risk.

It was wonderful to feel the freedom of being in charge of my own body again. Day after day passed with none of the symptoms the doctor had feared would manifest themselves.

Months went by. The pain that had troubled me in my back and joints disappeared completely. My spine straightened out, too, as the curvature righted itself. After years of painful limping, at last I could outrun my teenage sons.

I am still required to go back to both hospitals for check-ups once a year so that they can monitor my progress. The staff marvel that I'm so well despite not taking any drugs.

'You're doing fine, Mr Reynolds,' they say. 'You're in a period of remission.'

I understand that they don't feel able to acknowledge what God has done. Doctors are by nature a cautious breed when it comes to accepting that a miracle has taken place.

All I know is that my remission is eternal. It began four years ago when I resolved to trust God, quite literally, with my life.

2

'Even the grass has stopped moving'

Paul Croall, Wolverhampton

I knelt on the grassy slope and looked in wonder at a sight I'd never seen before. There, in minute detail, were individual spiky blades of grass.

I stumbled on, dazed with shock, stopping again to stare at other amazing sights. The bark on a tree, the stitches on my knitted sweater, even the pores on the back of my hands.

Where previously I'd seen only a shifting, velvety blur, the contrasting textures now showed up clearly in sharp relief.

'It's really happened!' I thought excitedly. 'I've got to tell Mum and Dad.'

I hurried back across the field to find them, weaving my way through hundreds of tents and caravans. We, and the rest of our church, were camping at the Dales Bible Week in Yorkshire.

Mum and Dad were sitting in the caravan when I found them. I burst in through the door.

'I've been healed!' I announced breathlessly.

'You've been what?' they both exclaimed in astonishment.

'Healed!' I insisted. 'The letters have all stopped moving. Even the grass has stopped moving.'

They were speechless. We wanted to shout and hug each other, then tell the whole world about the miracle that had taken place. But at the same time it was a terrible shock.

I was fourteen years old. My whole life had been spent under the shadow of a learning difficulty diagnosed as dyslexia. All that time we as a family had been praying, asking God to heal me. Now that he had done it, we could hardly believe it.

But it was true. It had really happened that very morning as I stood in the meeting-tent with several hundred other teenagers, singing and worshipping God.

A great banner proclaiming *One Way with Jesus* was hung across the front of the marquee. As usual, the huge letters appeared to be moving up and down, swirling round and round whenever I looked at them.

But despite that distraction, God felt near, so I closed my eyes and concentrated on him. When I opened them, incredulously I realised that the letters had stopped moving. For the first time in my life I could see normally!

Dyslexia is a strange disability. It takes so many different forms. Some people have difficulty writing and using numbers; for others it's letters.

Even quite simple words are jumbled up or reversed. Ordinary skills like tying shoe-laces or catching a ball are developed late or not at all. Until recently, many teachers and doctors wouldn't even acknowledge that the problem existed. Instead, they branded sufferers as subnormal or lazy.

My mum realised something was wrong with me when I was still a small baby. While all the other mums proudly showed off their baby's latest achievement she watched anxiously, knowing I hadn't learnt a thing.

She waited, understanding that all children develop at different rates. But I was eighteen months old before I took my first steps and began to say 'Mama' and 'Dada'.

By the time I was into my third term at school it was obvious that something was very wrong. No matter how hard I tried, I made no progress in learning to read or write.

Usually, in Britain a child has to be seven years old before any remedial help can be arranged. Realising this, my teacher, Mrs Elliot, offered to give me extra lessons herself. 'I'm sure he's an intelligent boy,' she told my parents. 'He's never disruptive. He really tries hard to understand the work.'

So my parents took me to her home during the holidays and there, while my friends played out in the summer sunshine, I sat with my books.

Year by year, as I moved from one class to another I experienced a variety of reactions from my different teachers. Some, like Mrs Elliot, were sympathetic and helpful. They looked beyond my pitiful attempts to read and write, seeing my frustration and trying hard to find some area in which I could excel.

Others, dismissing dyslexia as an excuse for idleness, made my life a misery. I vividly remember the first day of each new September term, when I would meet the person who was to teach me for the next year.

'I expect you all to work hard,' declared Mrs Griffiths, one of my infant school teachers. 'You must try to do your best. I won't stand for any laziness.'

'Oh, no!' I thought, wildly. 'I'm really for it now!' Cramp gripped my stomach, twisting and churning it with tension.

I *did* try hard. I tried my very best. I worked for hours after school, but with the letters shifting and moving around on the page my progress was excruciatingly slow.

'Lazy boy!' some teachers said. Would Mrs Griffiths understand? Or would she, too, blame me, punish me, allow the other children to snigger at my work?

Fortunately, she understood. She focused on my effort, not just my achievement, and tried as best she could to give me opportunities to develop.

But the uncertainty was there at the beginning of every school year. Thank goodness my parents understood. Home was a haven, a place where I could let off steam, chattering about my latest inventions or riding Saxon, my pony.

Unlike many parents of dyslexic children, my mum and dad never made me feel they were ashamed of me or of my disability. They went out of their way to make me feel loved equally with my brother, Barry, and sister, Ruth.

Barry was two years younger than me, Ruth four. I never realised at the time what pain it caused Mum and Dad to see them reading to their big brother. Their joy at Ruth and Barry's kindness towards me was marred by my need of their help.

But at school it was a different story. Being poorly co-ordinated at ball skills, I was shunned by the other children in the playground. I became a loner, standing against the schoolyard wall, always an onlooker, never able to participate. It was the loneliest time of my life.

One year, Mum and Dad arranged for me to join a group of children on a Warrior Camp in the summer holidays. Warrior Camps are organised by the Christian organisation, WEC International.

Mum and Dad knew there would be ball games, orienteering and quizzes. It was hard for them to expose me to the pressure of such a situation, but they realised I couldn't hide away at home. Some day I was going to have to go out into the world and stand on my own two feet.

The camp was very well organised, with a printed programme and private study notes. One evening, the leader taught us about how important it was to read the Bible.

'We'll be holding a Bible quiz competition,' he announced. 'Everyone who answers all the questions will receive a new Bible as a prize.' And he held up one of the smart new Bibles for us all to see.

How I longed to win one! But it was impossible. I knew the answers to the questions, but I simply couldn't write them down. Frustrated and upset, I burst into tears.

Joyce, the leader's wife, took me quietly to one side and, once she understood my problem, offered to hear me give my answers orally.

'Try to write them down, too,' she advised kindly. 'It doesn't matter how long it takes. Just let me have them when you've finished and you can have a prize, like the others.'

Two months after the camp ended I sent off the last of my answers, mostly misspelt, some almost illegible. But no-one was prouder than me to receive my prize – a brand new Bible!

I doubt if Joyce ever realised how much it meant to me to be able to win that prize. It was wonderful actually to achieve something for all my effort.

One other young man who helped me in a similar way was Ian, a leader at a camp reunion meeting. The children were split into groups, each with its own leader. I saw Ian deliberately choose to lead the group I was in.

Six questions were set, and the quickest way to get the answers was obviously for each person to take a different question, find the answer in the Bible and write it down. That's what every other leader decided to do.

'No,' Ian insisted, 'we work together as a team.' I knew he'd chosen to work that way to save me the agonising embarrassment of having to admit to the group that, at eleven years old, I still couldn't read or write properly. I was so grateful.

Our team came last. Amidst the grumbling of the rest of the team, who didn't understand why, and the jeering of a rather insensitive leader of the team next to us, Ian graciously took the blame. But he was my hero.

In September there was a change of school for me. I'd been seeing the school psychologist for some time and he'd recommended that I should go to Pembroke Secondary School, which actually had its own dyslexia unit.

We followed the normal secondary education syllabus, but with extra support. All English lessons were taught in the unit – maths, too, if a pupil needed it.

Despite having the dyslexia unit within the school, the ignorance among certain staff members was incredible.

'Totally unsatisfactory,' wrote one teacher beneath my attempt to describe a school trip. 'If there is no improvement in neatness, at least, by Christmas I shall punish you.'

Mum and Dad were furious. A visit to the school was necessary to put a stop to such negative remarks.

One weekend, Dad brought home a computer he'd borrowed from a friend. I was interested, despite all the words that appeared on the screen. Unlike television, where words flashed on and off at a frustrating speed, words remained on the computer screen no matter how long it took me to finish reading them. I could work at my own pace.

We were not particularly well off at the time. But, seeing my interest, my parents bought me a computer of my own. It opened up a whole new realm of possibilities for me. After hours of work, I was even able to exhibit some of my designs at a home computer users' exhibition in Ruislip Library.

At the end of my third year, my school report showed that I was top of the year for maths. Not just top of the dyslexia unit, but top of the whole third year! I began to dream of working with computers when I grew up. My lack of writing-skills made all other options extremely limited, but computers were a real possibility.

Imagine how I felt when I returned to school at the beginning of my fourth year, knowing that I'd been healed during the holidays! For the first time ever, I wasn't gripped by fear – I was just excited. I couldn't wait to get down to some work. Talking the situation over with Mum and Dad we agreed that it was best initially not to tell people about my healing.

'There are many teachers who've spent a great deal of time and effort helping you,' Dad advised. 'Don't rush in and tell them you don't need them anymore. Let them have the joy of seeing for themselves how much you've improved.'

He was right. It wasn't long before my new ability was spotted. My February report read: English language B+, maths A-.

July was even better: English language A-, maths A-, chemistry B, biology B. Comment: 'It is clear that Paul has made considerable efforts in all his subjects, with satisfactory results. A very good year's work. Well done!'

It was only the beginning. Pupils in the dyslexia unit were never entered for the English language CSE exam, and certainly never for English literature. So my parents were astonished when they received a phone call from school asking if I could be entered for both.

Because I hadn't been entered at the same time as everyone else, my parents had to pay separately for me to enter.

One of the ways the educational psychologist had helped was by having me made a 'subject of statement'. This meant that when I sat my GCE O level and CSE exams, the examination board would have someone beside me to read the questions and write down my answers.

But when the time came for me to take my exams, I knew I didn't need any help. I was grateful for the offer, but now that I could read and write perfectly well myself, I decided to turn it down.

I left Pembroke Secondary School at the end of my fifth year with a maths O level grade B, chemistry and pottery CSE grade 1, English language and English literature grade 2.

This was another miracle. None of my teachers expected me to obtain such high marks, particularly as I'd had to prepare for the exams in a much shorter time than the other pupils. The work had included writing five essays for the English language exam and fifteen for English literature.

Now things really started taking off. I transferred to Bucks College of Higher Education to study for a National B. Tech. diploma course in computer studies. One year into the course, the education authority wrote to my parents asking if I could be 'de-statemented'. I was now officially working normally.

My final year produced six credits in the six subjects and an overall distinction. This enabled me to obtain a place at Wolverhampton Polytechnic on the four-year Honours degree sandwich course. And there, at the Christian Union, I met Sue, whom I married in my final year.

I graduated with an Honours degree in computer science and won an IBM award for presenting one of the two top computing projects of the year!

Sue and I have settled in Wolverhampton where I work as a computer software engineer for a company in the Midlands.

NOTE

Paul Croall's story is told on video in *The Day the Grass Stopped Moving* (First Scene Productions). Available from video suppliers or from: Harvestime Publishing Limited, 69 Main Street, Markfield, Leicester LE6 0UT.

3

'I didn't realise how much God loved me'

Bill Fenna, Midsomer Norton

Becoming a Christian is the best decision I ever made. 'Gospel', the name given to the four books in the Bible which tell us about Jesus, actually means 'good news'. And God's incredible offer of a new start, a chance to be born again, was definitely good news as far as I was concerned.

My life was a mess, a total disaster, until the day I handed it all over to God and asked him to come into my life and change it.

It certainly needed changing. My marriage of seventeen years had just ended in divorce. In the bitter aftermath that followed, my business collapsed, plunging me into financial chaos and despair.

Anxiety heaped upon anxiety. Frazzled and weary, I struggled on, trying to get my life back into some sort of order. But eventually it was all too much for me to handle and I suffered a nervous breakdown.

Then God stepped in and things began to change. During the next two years I experienced a measure of peace and happiness I'd never known before. I joined the local church and made many new friends. And slowly, a new car sales business rose from the ashes of the old one as my finances came back into order. Things were looking up and life felt good.

'That's a bad cough you've got there, mate,' commented one customer at the garage as he paid his bill. I nodded weakly, trying to control the irritation in the back of my throat long enough to answer him.

The persistent cough that had been troubling me for some months was becoming a very embarrassing problem. It was difficult to talk to customers when I had to keep swallowing hard all the time to stop myself from coughing.

So far, I hadn't bothered going to the doctor about it. I didn't feel ill at all, and I just kept expecting it to get better of its own accord. But as the weeks went by and the coughing and spluttering continued, I decided to make an appointment to see my doctor.

I wasn't prepared for his reaction. He carefully examined my throat. Then, instead of reaching for his prescription pad as I had expected, he picked up the phone.

'I'm going to get you an appointment to see the ear, nose and throat specialist at the hospital,' he said. He rapidly made his request to the hospital receptionist.

'What is it?' I asked anxiously. 'What's the matter?'

'You have a small growth at the back of your throat,' he said. 'It's unlikely, but we need to check whether or not it might be malignant.'

'Malignant!' I cried in horror. 'Do you mean cancer?'

'I don't know at this stage, but it *is* possible,' he said. 'We really can't tell until you've seen the specialist. There's an enormous waiting-list for hospital appointments. You may have to wait as long as eight or nine weeks before you see him.'

Fear of cancer clutched my heart. I left his surgery with my mind reeling. A great surge of resentment welled up inside me.

'Why me?' I thought bitterly. 'I've had enough trouble in my life. And now, just when things are getting better, this has to happen!'

In my shock and misery at the apparently gloomy diagnosis, I forgot that when I became a Christian I'd put my life in God's hands. Foolishly, I took the whole weight of my dilemma on my own shoulders and sank into deep depression.

Why didn't I tell anyone what had happened? I could have talked to my family or the elders of the church. I could have prayed and asked for help or healing. Instead, I carried my burden alone for many weeks.

Day by day, the tension mounted as I scanned the post as soon as it arrived, hoping to find an appointment card from the hospital. But nothing came.

After nine weeks had gone by I went back to see my doctor again. He phoned the hospital immediately.

'Why hasn't this man received an appointment yet?' he demanded. I could see the frustration written across his face at the receptionist's reply.

'The waiting-list is even bigger now than when we first rang,' he said, putting down the phone. 'People are having to wait up to thirty-two weeks.'

Red-hot rage surged through me. 'I could be dead by then!' I screamed. I was afraid. I didn't want to die.

The doctor shrugged his shoulders helplessly.

'What if I pay to see the specialist?' I asked suddenly. I didn't know how I was going to scrape the money together, but desperately I reasoned that anything was better than finding that the growth had grown too bad to treat.

We rang the receptionist again. 'Yes, we could see Mr Fenna privately,' she agreed pleasantly. 'We have a cancellation on Wednesday next week. Would that be convenient?'

I accepted the appointment and saw the specialist at the clinic.

'There's definitely a growth there,' he said, peering down my throat. 'It's about the size of a large pea.'

I could feel the thing bobbing about in the back of my throat, causing me to cough and choke.

'I can't tell you any more until we've done some tests,' he said. He then made the arrangements.

The tests turned out to be a gruelling session of X-rays, including a barium meal. I felt apprehensive as the radiographer viewed my head and chest from every conceivable angle. But he was kind and reassuring as he worked.

'The growth shows up quite clearly,' he admitted.

My heart sank.

'We'll just have to wait for the X-ray results before deciding how to treat it,' he said.

That Saturday evening the church was holding a 'celebration evening' at Shepton Mallet. People from miles around came together to worship God and celebrate his goodness to them. I didn't feel much like celebrating, but I went along anyway.

Everyone was singing and clapping enthusiastically. I joined in outwardly, but inside I was really knotted up with anxiety.

Suddenly, the visiting speaker, Gwyn Daniel, stopped the music and came to the microphone.

'God has just told me that someone here has something wrong with their neck,' he announced. 'I'd like to pray for you.'

There was absolute silence. Two hundred people looked around expectantly to see who was putting their hand up, but no-one responded.

Gwyn spoke again. 'God has told me he wants to heal someone with a neck problem,' he insisted. 'Please put up your hand so that we can pray for you.'

I froze in my seat. No way did I want to be prayed for in front of all those people. In fact, the members of my own church still didn't know there was anything wrong with me.

'This is the third time I'm crying out to you,' Gwyn persisted. 'God wants to heal you. Please let me pray for you.'

Suddenly, inexplicably, my right hand shot up into the air. Gwyn spotted it and rushed across to where I was sitting. I couldn't help noticing that his microphone was still clipped to his tie and everyone in the room could clearly hear what we were saying to each other.

'What's wrong with your neck?' he asked.

'It isn't my neck,' I answered. 'It's my throat.'

Gwyn beamed at me good-naturedly. 'All right,' he said jovially, 'we'll pray for your throat. What's the matter with it?'

'I think I've got cancer,' I replied simply.

There was a gasp of shock and horror from the members of my family and church who were sitting nearby. The smile faded from Gwyn's face. He looked as if I'd just punched him in the stomach! But he didn't hesitate for a moment.

'OK, let's pray,' he said. He then laid his hands on me.

As he prayed, a warm sensation spread down my throat. It grew hotter and hotter. I began to choke and splutter. The growth in my throat seemed to swell horribly, filling the back of my mouth. I coughed and coughed, choking as I tried to spit it out.

Suddenly – I swallowed it! A look of pure astonishment spread across my face and Gwyn cried out, 'What's happened?'

'I've swallowed it!' I announced. 'I couldn't cough it up so I've swallowed it. It's gone!'

Everyone roared with laughter, and the praise and worship that followed was a great celebration. All I could do was sit in my seat, overwhelmed by the knowledge that God really loved me.

Of course, I'd known that before, but the

knowledge hadn't really touched me. I hadn't gone to God with my problems, confident that he loved me enough to take care of me. Instead, I'd worried and fretted and lost my temper, not realising that all the time God had everything under perfect control.

But the battle wasn't over yet. During the three days that followed, as I waited to see the specialist for the result of my X-rays, I fought a gloomy voice inside.

'You're not really healed,' it taunted. 'That lump may be gone but there'll be others.'

The specialist wasn't gloomy, just puzzled. 'I have your X-rays here,' he said thoughtfully. 'They're yours. I checked to be sure. But when I examine you now, I can find no trace of any growth, no scar tissue, definitely no sign of cancer.'

He was as thrilled as I was. 'There's only one way I can express how I feel about all this,' he said generously. 'I'm not going to charge you any fees for consulting me.'

I was very grateful but on reflection felt that he should be paid. After all, it wasn't his fault that God healed me before he could operate. I asked God for the money to pay the specialist and, miraculously, he provided me with it.

The knowledge that God loves and cares for me is still very special to me. With him involved in all I do, my business is flourishing in a way that is the envy of all similar businesses in the area.

I'm constantly aware of his goodness, of his personal interest in my life, especially now that I have a lovely new wife to share it with.

4

'Life will never be the same again'

Alisdair McKenzie, Inverness

I put my hand into my pocket and took out the aspirin I'd just bought. There was no going back now. I was going to take the lot. I didn't care if I died. Nothing could be worse than the misery of the life I had.

I'd been shoved from one children's home to another, whenever the violent relationship between Mum and Dad had erupted fiercely enough for the social services to step in. Day by day the tension inside me had mounted unbearably as I'd watched the arguments escalate. Finally, in an angry scene of shouting and hitting, Mum would walk out and leave us.

When, inevitably, Dad couldn't cope, a kindly social worker would call and find somewhere for us kids to stay until the storm blew over. Then Mum would come back and we'd return home – until the next big row.

'Not always the same home, either,' I remembered

bitterly. We were constantly in debt, the result of both parents being alcoholics. We simply upped and left when things got too hot, starting again somewhere else.

No wonder we four children stuck together. I was the eldest, and I was fiercely protective of my little sister, Dawn, and two young brothers, David and Scott.

Mum and Dad split up for good when I was twelve. This time Dad walked out and never came back.

We went to live with Dad when he set up home with another woman, Elizabeth. She already had two children of her own, Vanessa and Elizabeth. They were cute little girls, aged only three and four. And it wasn't long before there were two more babies, Donald and Paul.

Paul was a sickly baby, born with two holes in his heart. Doctors diagnosed the problem soon after his birth and we lavished him with special care and attention. But a blood vessel, swollen with extra pressure from his deformed heart, burst, flooding behind his eyes. Now, to add to his problems, Paul was blind in his right eye.

Dad got on better with Elizabeth than he had with Mum. Perhaps having a sick baby drew them together. They argued, of course, living in such cramped conditions with eight kids. And they kept on moving, rarely staying in one place for more than a year. But at least they remained together.

But I couldn't settle. I became wild and violent, drinking and experimenting with drugs. Sometimes, I'd try my hand at house-breaking – anything for kicks.

I hated what I was becoming. Everything I'd seen in my mum and dad, all the things I didn't want to be, were coming out in me. My life was following the same pattern, but I just couldn't change myself.

The last straw came when Dad and Elizabeth split up. My last shred of security was gone. I was eighteen years old and already so sick of life I didn't want to live. I bought the pills and hid myself away, determined to take the lot.

I swigged down the first handful with a glass of water. They tasted foul. I wondered what everyone would think when they found me dead. Would they care? Maybe David, Scott and Dawn would. I always looked after them when things got rough.

Until that moment, I hadn't really thought of how my suicide would affect them. Their pain and bewilderment would probably add to the insecurity they already had to cope with. I hesitated, the tantalising dream of escape from my circumstances vying with the responsibility I felt towards my brothers and sister.

'I can't do it to them,' I thought, shoving the bottle of pills into my pocket reluctantly. I walked back out of the room to rejoin the living, not telling anyone how close I'd been to ending it all.

But if I was going to live, I knew I had to get away from home and start a new life for myself. I needed food, clothes and shelter. Looking around at the grim job situation in my native Scotland, I decided the best thing to do was to join the armed services.

The Air Force accepted me, offering a place on an electronics course. I was ordered to begin my basic training in three months' time, at the end of October. In the meantime, I applied for live-in work in a hotel in Inverness.

I was too impatient to see if I had actually got the job, so I set out for the city. On the first night I had to stay at a Salvation Army hostel. I lay on a rough bed in a dormitory full of tramps and drop-outs. In the morning, after lining up for my hand-out of food at breakfast time, I set out to explore.

I was hanging around outside the Wimpy Bar, hungrily sniffing the hamburgers I couldn't afford to buy, when a crowd of young people turned up. They had a questionnaire and were chatting with the passers-by.

I was a sitting duck. One couple introduced themselves as Tony and Diana and straight off started asking awkward questions.

'If you met God today, could you give him one reason why he should allow you to go to heaven?' Diana asked.

I couldn't.

Tony opened his Bible and showed me where it says that God loved me enough to die for me. 'You need him, Alisdair,' he said. 'Why don't you ask him to change your life?'

I felt hot and uncomfortable. 'I think I'll try the Air Force first,' I joked feebly.

Before they let me escape, Diana shoved a leaflet into my hand. 'This is our phone number,' she said. 'If you ever want to talk again, just ring us up.'

I didn't know it then, but the crowd of young people were members of a GO! Team. They'd given up their jobs to spend a year telling people about God. What I *did* know was that I'd never seen people who looked more alive and enthusiastic.

Two days went by, and I couldn't get them out of my mind. Eventually, I rang the number on the leaflet.

'Alisdair, it's great to hear from you,' came the welcoming reply. 'Sure you can talk. Come round now, if you like.'

'OK, I'm on my way,' I said. I set off to walk the short distance to the address they had given me, when suddenly I felt a fool.

'What can God do for me?' I thought.

I walked for two hours arguing with myself. 'These people are nuts! God isn't interested in someone like me,' I told myself. And yet, there was something about them that provoked me. I might reject their God, but I wanted to be like them.

I telephoned again, half expecting a mouthful of abuse for keeping them waiting.

'Don't worry about it,' said Tony. 'We're just about to have a meal. Why don't you join us?'

I could hardly believe my luck. Boy, was I hungry! I rushed round to the house with no messing about this time and wolfed down everything they put before me.

It was a hilarious evening, full of terrible jokes and good-natured teasing. These kids didn't need drink or drugs to get high. They were just naturally full of fun. I'd never met anyone like them.

In the midst of all the laughter, Tony turned to me. 'Can we pray with you, Alisdair?' he asked.

'Pray?' I thought, aghast at the idea. 'What on earth do they want to start praying for?'

They gathered round and laid their hands on me. I felt so silly!

Suddenly, the feeling left me as I began to shake from head to foot. Unperturbed, the team continued to pray. Panic spread through me. What was happening? I wanted to run, to get as far away as possible.

The shaking was now uncontrollable. My knees collapsed and I fell to the ground. Then, all the fear and fight vanished as an amazing feeling of peace flooded right through my body.

'Oh, God,' I whispered, and a great torrent of words poured from my mouth in a language I'd never heard before.

'He's being baptised in the Spirit,' someone murmured in the background. But I didn't understand. I only knew that all the bitterness and hurt of the past was being washed away as I lay there on the floor.

What a wild celebration we had when the moment had passed and I could stand shakily on my feet again! I was lit up like a light bulb! Now I knew what the team had meant about being born again. I was a completely new person. And I couldn't wait to tell the whole world.

Every day, as soon as work at the hotel was finished, I joined the GO! Team on the streets and told the people passing by what God had done for me.

One day, as we stood handing out leaflets, my sister passed by. 'Hi there, Dawn,' I called.

She spun round and stared, hardly able to believe her eyes. I took her for a cup of coffee and together we began to catch up on all the family news.

'Elizabeth's come home,' Dawn told me. 'She and Dad have heard that you've gone all religious. They're wondering how long it'll last.'

'I haven't gone religious,' I insisted. 'It's much more than that. God's changed my whole life.'

I watched her smile in disbelief, and I couldn't blame her. Anyone who had known me before would be sceptical at the idea of my changing for the better.

'It's about time I went home for a visit,' I decided. Dad and Elizabeth had moved again, but I caught the bus and soon found them.

The house was different, but the atmosphere wasn't. The tension and insecurity that had ruled my childhood was still there. But somehow it had lost its power over me. Less than three weeks had passed since the last time we were together, yet I felt completely detached, so different from the people in the room that I might have been a stranger.

'I've come to pray for Paul,' I blurted out. 'God's going to heal him.'

There was a great guffaw of jeering laughter. 'Don't be a fool!' sneered Dad.

I ignored him and picked up my eighteen-month-old brother. I put my hand over his blind eye and he lay passively against me. Then I covered his good eye and he began to scream with panic, fighting and kicking.

He had always done that. The doctor used to test his sight that way. 'A baby, blind in one eye, will always struggle if you cover up his good eye,' he informed us.

So he was still the same. I laid my hands on him, as I had seen the GO! Team members do, and began to pray. The room was silent.

Paul sat quietly on my knee, too young to realise what I was doing. I put my hand over his good eye and waited. Nothing happened. No kicking, no struggling or screaming, just peace.

Looking down at my baby brother, who sat gazing around the room with his previously blind eye, I realised that he could actually see!

Dad and Elizabeth grabbed him from me and began to test his eye.

'You'd better take him to the doctor,' I said, dazed with shock. 'Tell him God's healed his eye.'

I walked out of the door, shaken to the core by the miracle I'd just witnessed. As the days went by, I waited impatiently to hear what the doctor would have to say.

The baby was healed. There was no doubt about it. Dad and Elizabeth said nothing about my praying for him, yet the doctor confirmed that Paul could definitely see out of his previously blind eye.

'Occasionally, a damaged eye will improve slightly over a period of years,' he said. 'But complete and instant restoration isn't possible.' And yet, the impossible had happened.

Dad, Elizabeth and Dawn are still highly sceptical. They admit Paul is no longer blind. The evidence can't be ignored. 'It must be a coincidence,' they insist.

But Scott and David were eager to know more and they, too, have become Christians.

I never did join the Air Force. Life was far too exciting in Inverness for me to want to go away. When I started my 'temporary' job at the Caledonian Hotel I had to explain to my new boss, David, that I was no longer able to work on Sunday mornings. A new church was starting in Inverness as a result of the work the GO! Team had done, and I wanted to be part of it.

Intrigued, David came along to a meeting and he, too, became a Christian. The church now meets each week in one of the hotel reception rooms.

The year went by and the time came for the GO! Team to return home and pick up the threads of their various careers. We were all sad to see them go. They'd been with us for such a short time, yet they'd built from scratch a strong, thriving church. For those of us who met God through them, life will never be the same again.

But a new team arrived that September, eager to carry on where the others had left off. And no-one was more thrilled than me when I was asked to be part of it!

5

'I thought I'd never see my mother again'

Ann Deakin, Manchester

I watched as the nurses and orderlies, already in their theatre clothes, wheeled the trolley on which my mother lay, down the corridor to the operating theatre.

Tears filled my eyes and a great lump rose in my throat. My husband Graham put his arms around me and held me close.

'Don't worry, Ann,' he said, reassuringly. 'She'll be all right.' But even as he spoke, we both knew that her chances were very slim.

We'd been woken at six that morning by the telephone ringing. Sue, my twenty-one-year-old sister, was in a state of panic.

'Mum's ill, Ann,' she blurted out hastily. 'I've rung the doctor and he won't come to see her. He wants me to take her to the surgery later, but she needs to see him *now*.'

I felt indignant. My mother was a lively lady of

sixty-five. Like many of her generation, she was always reluctant to 'trouble the doctor'. So I was certain that if she'd asked for him to visit her urgently, she really needed him.

'Ring him back,' I said firmly. 'Tell him if he doesn't come round straightaway he'll have me to answer to!'

The doctor arrived within minutes.

'Oh, my God, we'll have to get her to the hospital,' he said when he had examined her. 'I'll phone for an ambulance straightaway.'

Sue rang back to tell us the news and we drove swiftly from London to my parents' home-town of Bristol, where Mum had been admitted to Southmead Hospital.

'Thank goodness you've come,' exclaimed the anaesthetist with relief as we walked through the ward door. 'We have to operate immediately and no-one will sign the consent form.'

Sue stood tearfully beside my father. Both were too shocked and afraid to sign the form, knowing that there was a good chance Mum wouldn't come out of the operation alive.

Mum was in great pain. No matter what the risks were, we had to let the doctors find out exactly what was causing it. So, gently, I persuaded her to sign the consent form herself.

'Can we just have five minutes alone with her?' we asked.

The anaesthetist hesitated. 'OK. But only two minutes,' he said, and left us behind the screens.

Mum had already been given her premed injection so she was becoming too drowsy to talk much. We knew she could still hear us clearly so we prayed for her. Then the hospital staff came in and wheeled her away down the long corridor.

She looked so small and frail. As I watched her disappearing into the distance, I felt as if my heart would break. I loved her so much and I didn't know if I would ever see her alive again.

We waited for what seemed like ages, prowling up and down the corridor, then huddling uncomfortably on the hard seats. Wondering, hoping, praying that the doctor's depressing diagnosis would be proved wrong.

Hour after hour ticked slowly by. Time seems to stand still on such a tragic occasion, as if everything were happening in slow motion. But eventually the doctor arrived.

We jumped up anxiously, trying to read his face as he walked towards us.

'It's not good news, I'm afraid,' he admitted. 'We've opened her up and, as we expected, found a very large cancerous growth. It's completely blocking her lower bowel.'

My stomach churned at the thought of the pain and suffering Mum had ahead of her. I worked in hospital management and over the years had seen many people sick with this kind of cancer. It's a horrible way to die.

'Could you do anything for her?' I asked helplessly.

He shrugged his shoulders expressively. 'We daren't touch it,' he said. 'But the top part of her bowel is still intact so we've put in a simple colostomy which will make her more comfortable.'

'How long has she got?' asked my Dad shakily. The doctor shook his head gloomily. 'It could be seven days, seven weeks, seven months, even seven years, I suppose,' he replied.

Despite the severity of her condition, Mum recovered slowly and went home to be with Dad. We watched and prayed as two years went by without further major crisis.

Mum was still very ill, but she was a determined lady who wasn't going to give up without a fight.

We'd moved house by then and were living in Buckinghamshire. We invited them to come and stay with us and our three children – Andrea, aged eight,

Neil, six, and baby Gavin.

It was a difficult time. Mum was so ill that the doctor gave her an unlimited supply of very strong pain-killers.

'Just take them as often as you need to,' he said.

Graham and I knew the significance of such directions. On top of that, we could see her deteriorating rapidly. We had to face reality and, unknown to her, began discussing the arrangements we would have to make if she died before Mum and Dad could return to Bristol. It really did seem almost inevitable.

Early one morning, Graham awoke and felt sure that God was telling him to go to Mum's room and pray for her. We'd prayed for her before but never with the sense of urgency and faith Graham felt now.

He was a bit apprehensive at the thought of waking her up at the crack of dawn with such an odd request, so he woke me up first.

'Go and ask her,' I said. 'I'm sure she won't mind.'

Mum, slightly bewildered by this early morning visit from her son-in-law, nevertheless readily agreed that he could pray for her. Graham sat on the edge of the bed and began to pray.

As he prayed, a great anger at the thought of this dear old lady ending her days in such pain and distress overwhelmed him. He prayed firmly, taking the authority a Christian has over sickness and commanding it to go. When he had finished, peace descended and Mum smiled at him.

She felt better, and a few days later she and Dad were ready to return home to Bristol.

We were delighted to see her feeling better and cheerfully waved them off. But two days later she was on the phone, absolutely panic-stricken.

'Ann, something's wrong,' she cried. 'There's a lump in my back passage. I can feel it.'

'Go straight to the hospital,' I advised, sick with apprehension. I felt confused that such a thing should happen now, of all times.

Mum returned to Southmead Hospital and was examined immediately. The doctor was astonished at what he found.

'That isn't cancer you can feel,' he exclaimed. 'I can't find any trace of it at all. The lump you can feel is faeces. Your bowel is actually working normally.'

The impossible had happened!

Isn't it amazing? We pray to God for healing, but when he does what we ask we can hardly believe it. The cancer had gone. The doctor who had performed the colostomy now offered to reverse it.

It was a hard decision for Mum to make. She was sixty-seven by now. As the cancer had gone, there was no reason why she shouldn't get strong and well again. The thought of having to undergo a merely cosmetic operation to remove the colostomy didn't appeal to her.

'I'll stay as I am,' she decided firmly. 'I've been through enough without starting again.'

Fourteen years have gone by since we were first told Mum had perhaps just weeks to live. A consultant geriatrician gave her a complete medical four years ago when she spent two weeks at a private hospital being thoroughly examined.

'Well, Mrs Bobbet,' he declared, 'I can definitely find no trace of cancer at all!'

6

'God told me to get up and walk'

Esme Burt, Blackpool

Walking was something I hadn't done for a long time. About twenty years, in fact.

I used to be a very active person. I was a trained nurse and, as everybody knows, nurses rarely have time to stand still, let alone sit down. But I sat for over twenty years in a wheelchair.

I was working in a geriatric hospital at the time of the accident that changed my life so completely. I loved caring for the old people, even though the work was heavy and demanding.

As I helped them wash and dress, heaved them in and out of their wheelchairs, sat them on the toilet, I little dreamed that soon other nurses would be doing the same for me.

As well as caring for the patients, there are always plenty of other jobs to do on a hospital ward. When I saw that the tiled walls in the sluice-room needed cleaning, I got out the step-ladder, filled a bucket full of hot, soapy water and set to work.

Suddenly, I slipped. Before I could stop myself, I crashed heavily down on to the hard stone floor, twisting my back awkwardly as I fell.

The pain was excruciating. Nursing staff rushed from all directions and helped me to my feet. But I could barely stand.

One of the doctors examined me. 'It's bed rest for you, I'm afraid, Esme,' he pronounced gloomily. 'You're going to be off work for a long time.'

I'm glad I didn't realise then that I would never work again. I felt depressed enough as I lay in bed thinking about the long days of idleness stretching endlessly before me.

Weeks went by, filled with loneliness and boredom. I longed just to get up and walk away from the pain, to pick up the threads of my disrupted life. But the longed-for improvement never came. At the end of the extended period of bed rest, my back was as painful as the day I injured it.

I couldn't bend or stretch. I could hardly walk a step, shuffling instead from bedroom to bathroom and back again. I was only forty-five but as stiff and bent as the old ladies I used to care for.

The consultant at Bradford Royal Infirmary examined my back again. 'You've damaged your lumbar vertebrae,' he said. 'One of the discs is prolapsed.'

I knew then that it would be an uphill struggle ever to get back to the work I had previously enjoyed so much.

The spine is made up of thirty-three small bones, or vertebrae, which are stacked one on top of the other. In between each bone is a small disc of cartilage which prevents the bones rubbing together and acts as a shock-absorber when we walk.

When a disc is prolapsed, it is squeezed out of place and soon becomes badly worn as the body-weight crushes the bones together. The consultant recommended plaster traction in an attempt to put the disc back into place before too much damage was done.

I was admitted to Woodlands Orthopaedic Hospital on a fine spring day in May. As we drove down the long, winding lane that led to the hospital, the surrounding woods from which the hospital took its name were bursting with new leaves and blossom. The fact that I was about to be shut up inside the ward felt to me like a prison sentence.

I was encased in plaster from my armpits to my thighs, and lay flat on my back to enable the attached weights and pulleys to stretch out my spine and ease the disc back into place.

It was the first of many unsuccessful treatments and operations I endured over the following years, the most heartbreaking disappointment being a failed laminectomy.

This was an operation that I knew carried many risks and had only a fifty-fifty chance of being successful. But I was so desperate after four long years of constant pain that I was willing to try anything.

The surgeon opened my spine and carefully removed the crushed and battered disc. In some cases, removal of the disc brings considerable relief from pain. But I was left unable to walk at all and confined to a wheelchair.

'I'm sorry, Mrs Burt, but there's nothing more we can do for you.'

With the consultant's words ringing in my ears, I left for St Anne's Convalescent Hospital in Blackpool.

Gradually, I came to terms with the fact that I would never work again. My only source of income, a disability pension, although very welcome, served only to underline the fact that I was now officially a cripple.

As the years went by I reluctantly adapted to my circumstances. Rather than return to Bradford, I applied for and was given a warden-assisted flat in Blackpool.

A home help came to do my shopping and housework. Unable to walk even to the bathroom, I had a bed and commode in the lounge and lived in just one room.

Four community nurses came throughout the day and night. They washed and dressed me each morning and came back at regular intervals throughout the day to sit me on the commode. Each evening the night nurses came to put me to bed.

To help support my weight when I stood up to transfer from bed to chair or chair to commode, I had a Zimmer frame. One day, the pent-up frustration I felt at my helpless state built up to bursting-point.

'If only I could do something for myself!' I thought. I longed to stand up, to simply walk around the room as any normal person could.

The Zimmer frame stood tantalisingly beside my chair. Rebelliously determined to attempt some sort of independent feat, I painstakingly heaved myself to my feet.

My legs refused to move. As I struggled to walk even one or two steps, I fell and, with a sickening crack, broke my femur near the hip joint. It was back to hospital for a total hip replacement. Now I had more pain and less independence than ever.

Life settled down into a dull routine. Retirement age came and went. Any forlorn hope I might have secretly cherished of being well again died with each increasing year of confinement to the wheelchair.

Then, when I was sixty-eight, the most astonishing thing happened to me.

For two years I had been buying quite a few groceries from the home shopping service. The business was run by two young men, Simon and John. Every week they drove their van from house to house, a lifeline for the elderly and disabled. For me, housebound and lonely, their visit was a highlight in my dull routine.

Along with the groceries, they brought a breath of fresh air and a glimpse of the outside world I was so cut off from.

One week, they invited me to go to Blackpool Community Church, a church with a difference! The people were so kind and helpful. Each week they collected me and drove me to the community centre where the church met. They always wheeled me in my chair near to the front of the meeting so that I could see what was happening. And there was always plenty going on.

Everyone sang with great gusto the lively choruses, clapping and dancing around the room. Then, suddenly, the mood would change. Weeping, kneeling, reverently singing songs of love to God, a beautiful wave of worship would rise. I had never experienced anything like it.

It was obvious that these Christians had a wonderfully personal relationship with God. I wanted it, too. So they prayed with me and, immediately, my life was turned upside down.

A week later, the church was holding a series of special meetings. It was August Bank Holiday, and a barbecue was organised in the grounds of the community centre.

There were many visitors that day. First we had our usual worship time outside on the grass. After about an hour, Tom Rowley, the pastor at the time, invited anyone who wanted to be prayed for to walk out to the front of the meeting.

As I sat in my wheelchair watching, a voice inside my head spoke clearly to me. 'Get up, Esme. Get up and walk out to the front.'

Despite being such a new Christian, I knew for certain that God was speaking to me.

'I can't,' I replied. 'I can't walk.'

'You can do it,' the voice persisted. 'Get up and walk out to the front.'

A tremendous battle raged inside me. The voice of logic argued fiercely that to walk was impossible. Yet the voice of God continued quietly commanding me to do so.

With a Herculean effort I broke through the doubt that pinned me to my wheelchair, and rose to my feet. My legs, weakened by long years of disuse, shook and stumbled as I walked across the grass to where Tom stood.

His face was a picture, a mixture of incredulity and delight! I could see him hovering anxiously, ready to leap forward if I fell. But I made it, and the whole church cheered.

When I got home that night I put the wheelchair away in a cupboard. I didn't ever want to see it again. And it's still there, three years later.

The nurses were amazed when they came to put me to bed and I told them what had happened. But as the weeks went by they watched with delight as I grew stronger and stronger.

Since my legs were still very weak, I used my Zimmer frame to help support me. But soon I needed only walking-sticks. Today, I walk confidently with no help at all.

I rarely see the nurses who took such good care of me as I'm quite capable of looking after myself now. Occasionally, I bump into them when I'm shopping in town and they never cease to marvel at the change in me.

Tom recently asked one nurse, Shirley, what she thought about my healing.

'I only ever used to see Esme when she was in bed,' she said. 'But you won't catch her in bed very often these days. She's far too busy visiting friends and going to weddings!'

I've rearranged my home now. I moved the bed back into the bedroom and got rid of the commode.

Margaret, my home help whom I've known for fifteen years, is absolutely thrilled. 'It's a miracle,' she exclaims. 'It's far more than just being able to walk. You've got so much more confidence. You're a completely different person. When I come to visit you these days, you put the kettle on and make me a cup of tea!'

7

'My weeping's turned to dancing!'

Chris Youngman, Heswall

Dr Billington gazed at me impassively from behind his cluttered desk as I described to him the mysterious illness which had doomed our family holiday to failure.

Severe flu-like symptoms had brought our holiday to an abrupt end. But instead of getting better when I returned home, I grew weaker every day.

'You need a long rest,' said the doctor decisively. 'I'm going to sign you off work for a month.'

I could hardly believe the change that had taken place in my life. Me! Lying around the house, barely able to sit up long enough to eat! People marvelled at the amount of energy I usually had. I not only held down a demanding job as a physiotherapist, I led keep-fit classes, too.

But two weeks of gruelling tests at our local hospital, although eliminating many possible causes of my illness, failed to discover what was actually wrong.

The next few weeks proved even more distressing. First the liver specialist on the intestinal unit gave me a thorough going over. Then the blood specialist began. He mixed samples of my blood with radioactive chromium and reintroduced it into my bloodstream.

'I never thought I'd be radioactive!' I said jokingly. By now I had very little left to joke about. Black circles ringed my sunken eyes. My head constantly fell forward on to my chest, and my skin had turned yellow.

I was desperate to be well again. I felt willing to do anything to regain my old vitality and strength. When the specialists referred me to a psychiatrist I didn't mind at all. I didn't care what was causing the problem. I just wanted to be rid of it.

My search for health led me into many extra-ordinary practices. One friend, Sheila, brought me a hypnosis tape, designed to help those suffering from depression.

'I don't feel depressed,' I insisted. 'It's my body that's sick, not my mind.' But as soon as she left, I sat down to listen to it.

Susan, another friend, came regularly to massage the palms of my hands and the soles of my feet, using a technique called 'reflexology'.

I bought a book on mind over matter. 'If the doctors can't cure me, I'll cure myself,' I decided.

Throughout the Christmas holiday I lay on the sofa meditating, even practising psychic communication, with some degree of success. The possibility of these strange spiritual practices being questionable or dangerous never crossed my mind.

Months went by and, despite my weekly visits to the psychiatrist, fear was taking hold of every part of my life, so much so that I became more afraid of living than of dying.

I made up my mind that on my next visit to the

hospital I would climb to the top of that enormous multistorey building and throw myself off.

I told no-one of my plans, but Dr Billington, my family doctor, sensing that something was terribly wrong, called to see me one morning. And I confessed my feelings to him.

'I'm so frightened, doctor,' I wept. 'All I can think about is killing myself!'

No sign of shock or surprise showed on his face. Gently he explained that the best possible thing for me at that time was to be admitted to the psychiatric unit as an in-patient.

My days in the psychiatric unit were filled with unimaginable horror, panic and helpless sobbing, my nights terrorised by violent nightmares.

'This isn't real. It can't be happening to me,' I thought wretchedly. 'I don't belong here. I'm ill physically, not mentally.'

I couldn't understand what had happened to change me from a cheerful, intelligent woman, determined to get well, into a panic-stricken creature, lost for periods of time in a grey blankness of numb depression.

Days turned into weeks. Patients came and went, but I remained. Then, after six long months, my husband heard a radio programme about food allergy.

Peter was up a ladder at the time, decorating the front room. When he heard how ill people become when allergic to dairy foods, he rushed round to see Dr Billington.

'She's not *still* in the unit, is she?' gasped the doctor in astonishment. He swiftly arranged for me to see Dr King, the allergy specialist, at the Royal Liverpool Hospital.

I was ushered into his consulting room, where he sat behind his desk, flanked on either side by doctors, students and several nurses.

'You're my last hope,' I sobbed. 'I wish I were

dead!'

'Many people have come to me as their last hope,' he said encouragingly, 'and they are now well.'

I spent my second Christmas since I had become ill on Dr King's unit at the hospital. His restricted diet was helping, but the hoped-for miracle simply wasn't taking place.

'Your wife is suffering from a rare disease called myalgic encephalomyelitis,' he informed Peter. 'We call it M.E. for short.'

So now we knew the truth. I was suffering from an incurable disease, so rare that many doctors barely acknowledged its existence. But I felt only peace as I heard the diagnosis. At least I wasn't a hypochondriac.

Peter and I went down by train to the M.E. Society's annual general meeting in London. The hall was filled with ghastly, pale people, collapsed in their seats, many wearing surgical collars to support their drooping heads.

Several research doctors spoke at length during the day, but their message could be summed up in one sentence: 'We are searching for a needle in a haystack.'

I was now officially an invalid, receiving invalidity benefit. I'd battled hard against accepting that I needed it, always hoping that I'd soon be well.

But Dr King, sitting on the end of my bed the last time I was admitted to his ward, shattered those illusions.

'I hope to get you better than you are now,' he said sympathetically. 'But I don't realistically ever see you working again.'

His allergy tests showed that only five foods remained to which I was definitely not allergic: potatoes, oats, sugar, apples and chicken or eggs. This was all I had left to survive on. I must filter my drinking water. And even comforting cups of tea and coffee were now a thing of the past. Only herbal brews were possible.

Encouraged by the doctors, we attempted a family holiday, taking our daughter, Sally, and my mother with us. My muscles were so wasted that I could hardly walk any distance at all. We had to bring a wheelchair with us to use whenever we went out. I remember the look on my mother's face as she tried not to show her feelings whenever I climbed into the chair.

'I've had a phone call from an old friend of yours,' my mother informed me not long after we got back home. 'Do you remember Joy Tyler?'

'You mean the girl who lived across the road from us when I was about ten?' I asked incredulously.

'That's right,' Mother replied. 'It seems she's one of these "born again" Christians now. Joy says God has told her he can heal you.'

'Oh, no,' I thought, 'I don't want anything to do with a religious nut!'

But despite my initial reaction, I went to four meetings with Joy. On one occasion I saw a lady healed of depression. All my medical training rose up immediately. 'I'd like to see her again in a month's time,' I thought sceptically, convinced that her transformation couldn't last.

But when I looked at her glowing face, how I wished it could have been me!

With the coming of the new year something died inside of me. I didn't care whether I lived or died anymore – the misery just had to stop.

Reaching into my bedside drawer, I took out the bottles of pills I kept there and shook some of each into my hand. With an overwhelming need to blot everything out, I swallowed them all.

Hours later, I awoke in the high dependency ward at the psychiatric unit. When Peter arrived, the doctor called him into his office for a long talk.

'I'm afraid we don't hold out any hope of your wife's condition improving,' he said. 'There's really nothing more we can do.'

Peter was at the end of his tether as he finally accepted that I was dying. He knew that if I didn't succeed in killing myself first, my ridiculous diet would finish me off. For my sake, he hoped I wouldn't suffer much longer.

Seeing his distress, Joy arranged for me to stay at her home, and cared for me lovingly until the suicidal urge receded.

But bitterness at my predicament held me in its grip. I'd been through so much, suffered so many tests, examinations, treatments. Yet I was more ill than ever.

One morning, I could hold in my feelings no longer. A tidal wave of red-hot rage and resentment poured out.

'I just hate everybody!' I yelled. 'They've all failed me.'

Even as I spoke I knew it wasn't true. The doctors had done their best. My family had loved and supported me throughout my long ordeal. No-one could have done more. Whatever would Joy think of me?

But far from being shocked, Joy was delighted at my outburst.

'Chris, all that hatred is poisoning your life,' she declared. 'But if you want him to, God can change your life – give you a new start.'

'I could certainly do with one,' I thought. 'My life's a disaster.'

Joy telephoned her friend, Liz, who hurried round to pray for me. I sat on the sofa between them and Joy got down to business.

'Before you can have a new life,' she said, 'you have to sort out the old one. That's why Jesus died on the cross. He took your punishment so that God could forgive you for all that hatred.'

She went on: 'You can have a new life, but first you need to ask God to forgive you for all the wrong things you've done.'

I prayed, asking God's forgiveness for it all. I abandoned everything, my hopes and ambitions, dreams and disappointments.

The moment I did it things began to happen. Like a great plant, uprooted, taproot and all, the depression tore out of my body and seemed to disappear up into the ceiling. Instantly, I was healed.

Then, like a mighty wind, came the presence of God, rushing inside me, filling me to overflowing with love and joy and peace of such intensity I felt on fire with the glory of it.

Liz and Joy sat speechless, watching my glowing face. I was speechless, too, in a state of utter bliss, feeling totally well for the first time in almost three years.

The next day Joy took me home to Peter. Incredulity, amazement and hope chased each other across his face as he gazed at me. I wasn't going to die. I was going to live, really live!

Great, fat tears rolled down his cheeks. 'It's over!' he whispered to himself, again and again.

Several days later, as I stood in the kitchen putting my special foods, pills and injections into a basket, a quiet voice said, 'You don't need those.'

I looked up to see who had spoken, but no-one was there. I was completely alone in the room, yet I distinctly heard a voice. Could it be God speaking to me?

The hospital sister had already warned me about trying to reduce my drug dosage without supervision. Now I was considering stopping them all instantly. Years of medical training urged me not to risk it. And yet, I knew I'd already experienced one miracle.

'If I'm healed I don't need them,' I decided. And I never took them again.

The expected withdrawal symptoms never materialised. What's more, I found I could eat anything I wanted with no ill effects at all. I revelled greedily in eating chocolate, beefburgers and other junk food. Soon I was using my chlorine filter-jug for watering the houseplants!

'This lady has been healed of depression which lasted for almost three years, and allergies so severe they prevented her from living a normal life,' announced Bryn Jones to the thousands of people gathered in Leicester for a 'Day of God's Power' meeting. I was so glad to have the opportunity to tell everyone what God had done for me.

'And what's more,' he went on, 'she's asked God to heal her muscles which wasted away so badly during her illness. And God is going to do it!'

Suddenly, as I sat among the worshipping congregation, my back jolted upright with a bang! It gave me a terrible fright. I stood up, my head held high with ease. And when I raised my arms in praise to God they shot into the air effortlessly – and they stayed up instead of flopping down! My head never hung forward out of control again.

Wild with excitement, I shouted praise and thanks to God at the top of my voice. I felt wonderful. Gladly, I wrote to the Social Security Office to tell them I'd been healed and no longer needed my invalidity benefit.

The following Monday evening I stood up as instructor of a keep-fit class for the first time in years. My leotard hung like a sack. It would be some time before I put back all the weight I'd lost. Hesitantly, I showed the class a warming-up exercise. Then I put on the music and watched them swing into action.

An incredible thing happened to me as I stood there. Power surged through me, strengthening my muscles as my body came to life. I leapt to the music, dancing, kicking, joining in the whole routine. Everyone stared at the amazing sight. One girl wept as she realised the significance of what was happening before her eyes.

News of my remarkable recovery swept through the town as reporters came to interview me for their newspapers.

'I'm baffled by Mrs Youngman's rapid recovery,' confessed Dr King, the allergy specialist, when the reporters interviewed him. 'She was in a very bad way and I wouldn't have expected her to get better for many years, if at all.'

Dr Johnstone, the kind psychiatrist whose care had saved me from killing myself, asked to see me. He sat in his office staring at the file crammed with case-sheets about my long illness.

Only a month ago he had told Peter that nothing more could be done to help me. Now I was bursting with life.

'Well, I don't think I need to see you again, do I?' he decided thoughtfully.

Thanking him for his help and support, I joyfully turned and walked out through the glass double-doors of the psychiatric unit for the very last time. Three years of hell were finally over.

NOTE

Chris Youngman's story, described by the *Chester Chronicle* as 'An addictive journey through the limits of human experience and the miraculous', can be read more fully in her book, *Holiday in Hell*, published by Harvestime.

A video has also been produced, *The Chris Youngman Story* (First Scene Productions). Available from video suppliers or from: Harvestime Publishing Limited, 69 Main Street, Markfield, Leicester LE6 0UT.

8

'It was one of the most fantastic experiences of my life'

Roy Jennings, Bath

The relief was indescribable, the peace wonderful, as everything that had tormented me for twenty-six years vanished instantly.

My nightmare began back in 1956 when my wife, Mary, and I were living in Balham, South London. We were a happy family with two small sons and a third child on the way.

At the time, I worked as a supermarket manager. It was a very demanding job in which I regularly worked seventy or eighty hours a week, carrying responsibility for the entire operation of the store.

We were Christians, heavily involved in raising funds to finance the running of the local Free Church of England. One of my projects was collecting newspapers, which we sold to a dealer as soon as we had enough to make up a good load.

Mary and I rented a flat in a large house. It had a garage with a loft above it, very useful for storing newspapers until it was time to take them to the dealer.

It was while I was putting newspapers into the loft that I met with my accident. One evening I was throwing bundles of them to my friend, fourteen feet above me in the loft. Engrossed in our work, neither of us noticed a heavy box teetering on the edge of the loft-opening.

I looked up at my friend, about to throw him the next bundle, when the box fell and smashed me in the face. Stars exploded all around me. Then I remembered nothing until I awoke the next day to find myself in hospital. I felt like I'd been hit with a telegraph-pole!

Some of my teeth were broken. I couldn't breathe through my nose and I had the most awful headache.

I also heard dreadful noises, banging and ringing inside my head, and the vision in my right eye was blurred. It felt like a nightmare. And as time went by it grew worse, not better.

Over the next twenty-six years I tried all sorts of painkillers in a desperate attempt to control the excruciating headaches. But there was only temporary relief as, steadily, the noises in my head increased in variety and intensity.

Insomnia held me in its grip. Night after night I sat up in bed reading until two or three in the morning, miserably conscious that I would have to be up at six to drag myself to work, more dead than alive.

The doctors could do nothing, and it didn't occur to me to ask my friends at church to pray for me. They were lovely people, but we would never dream of sharing our problems or praying for one another.

Five years went by. As the demands of my job became greater and my health didn't improve, we decided to move to Bristol. Hopefully, the pace of life in the sleepy south-west would be slower than London.

It *did* seem a little easier at first, but it wasn't long

before the pressure began to build up again.

My personality changed as I became aggressive and bad tempered. I would lash out at my family and colleagues, becoming very unreasonable and unpredictable in my anger.

We tried one church after another, of many different denominations. In our longing to find fulfilment in our relationship with God, we discovered only dull church services, jumble sales and committees discussing the upkeep of the building.

'Oh, God,' I cried, 'if this is all there is to the Christian life, then I quit!'

There were times when I felt sure I was going insane. 'I wish I was dead,' I moaned, reaching for the bottle of whisky. What started as a single drink to ease my pain slowly increased, until nothing less than half a bottle at a time had any effect.

Work was another escape. I changed my job to become managing director of a company, with my own secretary, a strong sales force and a good right-hand man.

I worked hard. I was a great success, making plenty of money for the company, involved in and committed to many important projects. Then one day my mind became a complete blank!

I sat in my office, staring at the walls in horror as I realised I couldn't remember what I was supposed to be doing. Fear clutched my heart. I had appointments to keep, work to do, and yet I didn't know what they were!

Suddenly, the telephone rang. Panic swept over me as I leapt to my feet, rushed out of the door and ran down the corridor. Hurriedly, I locked myself in the toilet and leant against the cool walls. Gradually, the panic subsided and I was able to return to my office.

But I was afraid. So afraid that I dreaded going to work each day. Finally, something snapped inside me. I had a complete nervous breakdown. In one day, everything I'd worked so hard to achieve collapsed in ruins.

For weeks I shut myself away at home, unable to force myself to go back to work. When I did return, I realised I could no longer cope, so I resigned.

My wife, Mary, who had loyally loved and cared for me through all the difficult years, asked me to try just one more church. 'This could be what we've been looking for,' she pleaded. So, reluctantly, I went with her to the Bath Christian Fellowship.

What a difference! There was life, love, caring and sharing – everything, in fact, we'd ever looked for in a church.

Suddenly, God was real. No more treadmill of boring services and jumble sales, but a whole new way of life. We sold our house and moved from Bristol to Bath so that we could be fully involved.

A year later, one cold January night, the church was holding a meeting at a school hall. It was called a 'celebration evening', and was exactly that. It was more like a party than a church service as crowds of people gathered together to celebrate God's goodness towards us.

The visiting speaker was Gwyn Daniel, leader of a similar church in Birmingham. Towards the end of the meeting he said, 'God wants to heal people of head problems and headaches.'

Immediately, God spoke to me: 'Roy, stand up and I'll heal you.'

I jumped to my feet and everyone gathered around and laid their hands on me. As Gwyn began to pray, the unbelievable happened. My headache vanished, the noises in my head stopped, all the banging, ringing and screeching that had tortured me for years simply disappeared!

I went home that night a completely different man. I still didn't sleep because the silence was so strange. So I lay awake whispering, 'Thank you, Lord. This is wonderful – and so are you.'

Nine years have passed since that night. Many things have changed. My sons have grown up. Two are married and we have three little grandchildren.

The headaches have never returned. Instead of struggling to cope with a nightmare existence, I'm fulfilled and at peace, glad to be alive. I'm so very grateful to God.

9

'My friends thought I'd flipped when I claimed a miracle'

Audrey Clayton, Bradford

A miracle was all I'd got left to hope for. What can you do when someone you love is dying by degrees and doctors can offer no cure?

I hadn't been to church for over ten years. Somehow, I'd drifted away. But when the crisis came I turned back to God and found that he still loved me.

Because I've never married and had children of my own my nephews and nieces are especially precious to me. I've watched them growing up, been proud of them when they've achieved things, shared their happiness and their difficulties. The news that Peter, my niece's husband, was dangerously ill came as a tremendous shock to me.

Peter had been to a football match. He'd had a slight cold but had hardly noticed it as he stood on the terraces cheering his team that fresh April afternoon. When he got home, however, the slight cold turned into bad flu symptoms.

He took a couple of days off work and stayed in bed, expecting that the worst would soon be over. Instead, late one evening his illness took an alarming change of course.

Peter became delirious. His temperature shot up, his head ached. In a matter of hours he became so ill and confused he couldn't even recognise his own wife.

Jacqueline, of course, was very frightened and rang her doctor's deputising service immediately. A doctor arrived and examined Peter.

'Give him some paracetamol,' he said casually. 'Then ring your own doctor in the morning and let him decide what to do.'

Jacqueline was angry. As a trained nurse she knew that something was seriously wrong. 'It's just not good enough, doctor!' she insisted. 'My husband is extremely ill and needs to be admitted to hospital.'

Wearily, the doctor picked up the phone and made arrangements for Peter to be admitted to the medical ward at Bradford Royal Infirmary. The staff there began to investigate his illness and monitor its progress.

Throughout the next day the charts on the end of Peter's bed showed his temperature climbing dangerously high. He still didn't know Jacqueline but became increasingly confused. His head ached intolerably and he began slipping in and out of consciousness.

Suddenly, his body jerked wildly in a series of convulsions. Medical staff rushed to his side. 'We'd better transfer him to the intensive care unit,' decided the doctor, as the fits showed no sign of abating.

It seemed that one crisis followed another. Tests showed that Peter had an extremely rare illness, herpes encephalitis.

The herpes virus shows itself in several different ways. Herpes simplex is responsible for those painful cold sores that appear around the mouth. Herpes zoster produces shingles. In its rarest form, herpes encephalitis was causing Peter's brain to become sore and inflamed.

My heart was heavy when I heard this. I work as a nurse, too, and I knew from experience what could happen to patients who recovered from an inflammation of the brain. Even if they escaped actual brain damage, all too often they would suffer a complete change of character, becoming aggressive and moody.

Peter was such a lovely young man. He was clever, too, working at a very responsible job in the bank. For him to become brain-damaged or even die was unthinkable.

'Can nothing be done?' we asked over and over again.

'I'm afraid not,' the doctor replied gloomily. 'Over the past thirty years there have only been six cases of herpes encephalitis in Bradford.'

'Well, what happened to them?' we wondered fearfully.

'Three died,' he admitted. 'And I'm afraid the other three all suffered severe brain damage.'

Things went from bad to worse. A brain scan revealed that over half Peter's brain was affected. Day by day he grew weaker until one day he suffered a respiratory arrest. Now he couldn't even breathe by himself but had to exist on a life-support machine.

The thought of that previously strong and healthy man dying, and of my young niece distraught with grief, was too much to bear.

I cried out to God for answers. 'Why, God, why?' The situation seemed so hopeless. We always seem to believe that doctors have a cure for everything. If *they* can't help us, who can?

As I sat at home, anxiously thinking of all that the impending tragedy would mean to Jacqueline, the silence seemed oppressive. I don't usually listen to the radio much, but I needed to hear another voice, so

I switched it on.

Stevie Wonder was singing, 'I just called to say I love you, I just called to say I really care.' His words made a tremendous impression on me. I'd heard that song many times before, but today I needed to hear someone say those words to *me*. I needed someone to show that they loved and cared for me, someone to help me in my present difficulties.

'I must go back to church,' I decided. 'I need to be with God's people.' I remembered all the love and fun I'd shared ten years ago when I'd been a member of Church House Fellowship. How I longed to see the people there again!

It took me a few days to track them down. The church had grown enormously in my absence and they'd moved to a large, purpose-built building. They'd changed their name, too. They were now called Abundant Life Church, reflecting the goodness of God towards them.

There were so many new faces, I thought at first that I didn't know anyone at all from the old days. Then one after another appeared, squashing me in great bear hugs, exclaiming, 'It's good to see you again, Audrey.'

The service seemed tailor-made for me and my circumstances. It was as if God, having had to wait ten years to get me there again, had decided to make full use of the opportunity. When the speaker, Keri Jones, started to speak I could hardly believe my ears.

'I was in my car, driving up the motorway the other day,' he began, 'listening to Stevie Wonder on the radio singing, "I just called to say I love you."'

'I thought to myself,' he went on, 'that God does that for us. Sometimes, he calls to tell us that he loves and cares for us.'

I was so excited. Keri then talked about the apostle Peter walking on water. When Peter became afraid and began to sink, Jesus lifted him up and rescued him. When we feel afraid and overwhelmed by our circumstances, God will help *us*, too.

'Do you need a miracle?' Keri asked as the meeting drew to a close. 'Let's pray for you now.'

I put my hand up straightaway. Tears poured down my face. I'd been away so long, yet God still cared so much for me. I knew that he could heal Peter, so I told those who gathered around me all that had happened.

Old friends who knew me previously put their arms around me and we prayed together. Peace filled my heart and mind as I brought my problems before God and asked him to provide a solution where no-one else could.

When I went back to work later in the day, my colleagues, who knew how distressed I'd been about Peter's illness, were surprised to find me cheerful and optimistic.

'I've claimed a miracle,' I explained. 'We prayed for Peter at church today and I'm sure he's going to get better.'

There was a shocked silence. Four days ago I'd been devastated. Now I was talking confidently about God performing miracles. I got on with my work, conscious of the puzzled expressions on the faces around me.

'Poor old soul,' I could almost hear them thinking. 'The strain's been too much for her.'

But deep inside I was so certain that God was going to heal Peter that nothing disturbed my faith.

A month went by and, although there was no instant change, Peter's condition stabilised and he began to make progress. Little improvements turned into great victories. He recovered enough to be taken off the life-support machine, then to be transferred from intensive care back to the medical ward.

He was still confused, very ill and weak, and needing medication to control his fits. Despite his condition, the doctors admitted freely that they could do nothing more to help, so they discharged him.

Jacqueline's parents invited her and Peter to stay with them, and she accepted gratefully. She knew that caring for her husband would be a full-time job and she needed all the support she could get.

His memory was completely wiped out. Whenever I went to visit him he was very pleased to see me. But if I left the room for a moment and then returned, he had no idea I'd been there before. He didn't know what time of day it was, even whether it was day or night. He was as helpless as a baby.

We were thankful that he was alive, but it wasn't good enough. We wanted him fully restored to health, not a feeble shadow of the man we'd once known.

June the fifth was my nephew's wedding day. Jacqueline was to be a bridesmaid so, of course, Peter was invited. Because his condition varied from day to day we didn't know if he would be well enough to attend or if his parents would have to look after him. Friends – not just from our church but from others, too – prayed faithfully for him. When the day dawned, we were delighted to find that he was feeling especially well.

We look back now and see that day as a milestone pointing to a marked acceleration in his progress. Little by little Peter's memory returned. Day by day he grew stronger until we saw without a doubt his old personality emerging.

It's impossible to describe our joy when the doctor finally declared Peter fit enough to start work part time in July. His colleagues welcomed him back to his old job at the bank and within a month he was strong enough to return full time.

Doctors at the hospital, colleagues at work, friends and neighbours are amazed at the speed and fulness of his recovery. There's no sign of the personality disorder I'd feared would occur and he no longer requires any medication at all. For me to be part of the chain of events leading up to Peter's healing was an experience I'll never forget.

In sharing my problems with the church and receiving their support and encouragement, I realised that Christians aren't intended to set themselves apart. We need one another, not just at times of crisis, but day by day. I gladly became a committed member of the church again.

Two years on, I'm thrilled to be able to say that Jacqueline and Peter are now expecting their first baby. There's something wonderful about a young woman who faced only widowhood and a man who almost died, to be able to play their part in creating a new little life together.

10

'God healed our baby'

Rita Drakes, Boston

The news that we were expecting our sixth child came as a great surprise to my husband, Dave, and me. But as the baby grew inside me, the enormity of the miracle taking place also grew.

This baby was a gift from God, precious and special. It wasn't long before we were discussing names and looking forward to the new arrival as much as we had all the others.

When we realised that something was seriously wrong with our baby, we loved her and prayed for her all the more.

I had a routine ultrasonic scan at the local hospital which showed that the placenta was rather low lying. So a second scan was booked for the thirty-fourth week of my pregnancy.

It became a family outing, Dave and the children all crowding into the examination room with me. We watched in wonder as the picture of our baby began to appear on the monitor.

We saw her head, arms, hands and heart. We were enthralled, totally absorbed in observing this little creature, soon to become a noisy member of the family.

But something was wrong. I knew it! Where the baby's stomach should have been there appeared a large black mass.

I glanced at the doctor and his face betrayed his concern. He pointed out the mass to the midwife but didn't comment on it at all. With my heart in my mouth, I waited to hear what he would have to say.

'Er, well, Mrs Drakes, I think I need to see you again,' he said, trying to sound unconcerned.

I was aware of our young children clustered around us, oblivious to the tension in the room.

'The scan shows that your placenta is low, so I'd like to see you again in a month's time.'

We filed out of the examination room and went home, to wait and to wonder, but most of all to pray.

The moment we left the room, the doctor apparently turned to the midwife. 'I've never seen anything like that before!' he exclaimed. 'It could be a cystic mass or exomphalos.'

Exomphalos is an extremely serious condition in which the intestine and abdominal organs develop outside the baby's abdomen.

The midwife was a friend of ours. But quite correctly she kept her knowledge to herself at that time, only telling us of the doctor's remarks after our baby was born.

Three weeks went by. The time for the third scan was fast approaching. It's a wonderful thing to belong to a church like ours. You don't have to stand alone in times of difficulty. We went along to speak to the church leaders and they shared our concern for our unborn baby.

'We need to get the whole church in on this,' they agreed. 'We'll ask everyone to fast and pray until the baby's healed.'

During the next week the whole church stood by us, fasting and praying, calling on God to heal the baby, even while it was still in the womb.

At the end of the week, Dave wasn't able to go to the hospital with me for the scan appointment. He was recovering from a minor operation, so I went alone.

The doctor had a video camera ready in the examination room to record the scan rather than relying on the still photos they take routinely. I knew then that he was expecting to see something out of the ordinary.

His idea was to compare the scan picture with the baby's actual condition when eventually it was born. This would enable him to make a more accurate diagnosis in future cases.

I lay on the examination couch and watched with bated breath to see what would be revealed on the monitor.

As the scan was carried out, it quickly became evident that something had happened. The black mass had disappeared. The picture on the monitor clearly revealed a perfectly normal baby in my womb. The only thing the doctor could record was, 'No evidence of abnormality found'.

He could hardly believe it. 'Well, we shall see when the baby's born,' he remarked to the midwife after I had left the room.

It was wonderful to be able to report such good news to the church on Sunday morning. And in the evening meeting, as another baby was being dedicated, God began to speak to us through prophecy.

'As the enemy of souls is destroying life, even in the womb, in these days,' said the person bringing the prophecy, 'so I, the Lord, pronounce life in the womb from the moment of conception. And I pronounce life upon this child.'

Suddenly, I could see a picture of the battle God

had fought over me. God himself was declaring life on our yet-unborn baby. I felt tremendously encouraged.

With the blight which had threatened my pregnancy now removed, we waited eagerly for the great day when our baby would be born.

Esther Miriam arrived on 5 October 1982, a perfectly healthy child, although the birth was not without incident.

At an early stage in the delivery, the midwife noticed signs that the baby was distressed. When the head was delivered the cord was found to be wound twice around the baby's neck!

Our precious little girl, so fought for and prayed over, grew strong and healthy. Then, when she was six years old, we noticed some distressing signs that all was not well. Esther suddenly began to stare into space, her eyes rolling upwards. For as long as thirty seconds at a time she would be unable to communicate with us.

At first we thought she was being naughty. 'Don't be silly, Esther,' I'd say when she slipped into this trance-like condition. But it quickly became obvious that she wasn't being silly at all. This 'dream' could happen anytime, anywhere, up to a hundred times a day.

At Easter, we as a family had a day out with friends at a country park. While the children were playing in the children's area, Esther had one of her 'dreams'. Momentarily unaware of her surroundings, she walked straight in front of a swing and was hit by it. She wasn't badly hurt, but the implications of what had happened were quite far-reaching.

Obviously, her safety was at risk. We no longer dared let her cross even the quietest road on her own. And riding her bike outside the garden gate was strictly forbidden.

'I won't have a dream, Daddy, I promise. Please let me ride my bike to school again,' she begged.

I felt as if my heart was torn in two.

Our doctor diagnosed a mild form of epilepsy. Petit mal, he called it. He endorsed our bans and added that Esther mustn't use the physical education apparatus at school.

She felt the restrictions terribly, but accepted them as necessary. Every day she prayed, asking God to heal her so that she could ride her bike to school again.

Fortunately, Esther's teacher was very understanding. Her own son had suffered from the same problem.

'Don't worry,' she said encouragingly. 'She'll be all right as soon as you get her on to medication.'

But we were reluctant for Esther to become drug dependent. The consultant at our local hospital confirmed our family doctor's diagnosis. We sat in her consulting room and watched with surprise as she asked Esther to blow against her finger.

'This test normally provokes the symptom to manifest itself,' she explained.

Esther blew and blew with all her might. Silently, we prayed that nothing would happen. Just when the consultant was about to give up, there it was – Esther had a 'dream'.

'She'll probably grow out of this problem in her teenage years,' the consultant reassured us. 'But until then she should take the drug Epilim. It will enable her to lead a normal life.'

She referred us to the Queen's Medical Centre at Nottingham, where Esther would have to undergo a brain scan before any drugs could be prescribed for her.

Once again we took the problem to our church and asked them to pray with us about the situation. Visiting leaders encouraged us not to accept the disability but to trust God to heal her.

In August we went, along with the rest of the church, to the Bible Week at Builth Wells in Wales. People were being healed there of all sorts of sickness.

Day after day we waited expectantly to hear the news that Esther's 'dreams' had stopped. But they didn't. If anything, the condition was worse that week.

Our hospital appointment was scheduled for September. Esther underwent an EEG (electro-encephalogram) scan of her brain. It was heart-breaking to see such a little tot wired up to a machine, with electrodes stuck on to her scalp. But she didn't seem too anxious about it.

Back home, we returned with some trepidation to see the consultant at the local hospital. Several months had gone by since we last saw her, and she was amazed to discover that Esther was still not on any medication.

'We need to start her off on Epilim immediately,' she decided.

'What about any side-effects the drug might have?' Dave asked.

The consultant became evasive, but we persisted until she admitted that it could cause liver damage if taken long term. 'But, of course, we would take your daughter into hospital regularly to monitor any side-effects,' she said.

Dave and I looked at each another. We felt uneasy about the whole idea of giving a child drugs to mask one symptom, and causing side-effects that would produce a completely different set of problems.

'Esther has never even fallen down during all the months she's had this problem,' I said. 'I think I'd rather keep a close watch on her than risk putting her on drugs to mask her symptoms.'

The consultant agreed to our decision providing we brought Esther in for a check-up every three months. But from that day her condition slowly began to improve.

Only a few weeks later, in November, a visiting speaker came to our church. Gwyn Daniel, from Solihull, spoke on the subject of healing.

Some people were healed before our eyes during

the time of prayer afterwards. Esther was prayed for, too. But she wasn't one of those who showed an immediate, definite recovery. Instead, over the weeks that followed, two things happened.

First, Esther's 'dreams' diminished. Instead of many times a day, sometimes five or six in quick succession, they manifested themselves only occasionally.

The second changed factor was that now when Esther had a 'dream' she could be contacted and brought out of it. Her recovery continued until by the end of January she was completely back to normal.

Only on one occasion since then has Esther been troubled by a 'dream'. She was off school, early in the year, suffering from a throat infection. As her temperature climbed, the old symptoms occasionally returned. But as soon as she was well again, the problem petered out.

Although she is so young, Esther's belief that God would heal her never wavered. Throughout her illness she prayed faithfully for her own healing.

'Thank you, God,' she prays now. 'Thank you for making me better and that I can ride my bike to school again.'

11

'The dead cells are now alive'

Velda Beach, Potton

I'll never forget the day the hospital consultant said to me, 'The cells that were dead are alive again.' The evidence was plain for all to see. And yet he could hardly believe what he had discovered.

He read and reread the audiology report, trying to convince himself that there was a logical explanation for the miraculous restoration of my hearing.

'Stand up,' he commanded brusquely. He then peered into my ears with an auriscope. 'The cells must have been asleep,' he decided.

I tried hard not to laugh at his bewilderment. But how convenient that cells which had been asleep for twenty-seven years should suddenly decide to wake up precisely at the moment I was being prayed for!

I wasn't born deaf. I caught measles when I was seven years old and my inner ears were damaged.

For many years my mother took me to visit the Ear, Nose and Throat Hospital in Grays Inn Road,

London. They tried many different kinds of treatment, some very unpleasant. But nothing succeeded in improving my hearing.

When I was ten I was issued with my first hearing-aid and that raised my general level of hearing. I used it mostly for lessons and school assemblies as I could lip-read well enough to cope without it on a one-to-one basis.

I passed the eleven-plus exam and went to a local grammar school, but one day each week I attended a school for deaf children for regular help and assessment. Many of the children there were deaf from birth and so had never learnt to speak properly. I was very grateful for the hearing ability I did have.

I left school and worked for a few years before marrying Peter. We moved to Cambridgeshire when our first son, Daniel, was born. By this time I'd almost totally abandoned using my hearing-aid. Teenage vanity and lip-reading fluency had encouraged me to manage without it. The aid was big and ugly and I was very conscious of the wire that couldn't be concealed at my neckline.

When Daniel reached the crawling stage I had problems knowing what he was up to. The downstairs of our home was open-plan, the kitchen leading through the dining-room to the lounge. We had no way of closing off any room, and no view of the lounge from the kitchen.

Daniel was an adventurous baby, a constant climber. When he finally learned how to open the door to the hall I dare not let him out of my sight. Unlike other mothers, I couldn't hear the tell-tale rattle of the door handle to warn me that he was about to embark on the stairs!

The health visitor told me that as a young mum I qualified for a local pilot-scheme where I could be fitted with an invisible, behind-the-ear aid. I was referred to an ear, nose and throat consultant at Addenbrookes Hospital and was fitted with the aid during 1972.

I remember hearing lots of things for the first time – clocks ticking, the sounds my baby made in his sleep, birds singing in the garden. After an initial period of getting used to the aid, and with the help of a new longer-length hairstyle to cover it up, my deafness soon became the best-kept secret in the village.

Very few people even knew I was deaf, fewer still that I wore a hearing-aid. Only my family and a few close friends knew. Being deaf wasn't a problem to me. I was soon to discover that I handled being deaf far more easily than being healed.

We were members of a local church, and Peter was involved with the Full Gospel Business Men's Fellowship International. They held regular dinners in local hotels. Christians invited their non-Christian friends along for a good meal and to hear a speaker afterwards.

A dinner was arranged for 5 November 1979 so we and a couple from our church, Lester and Julia, went along. The couple didn't know I was deaf.

After the meal the speaker began to tell us about the things God had done in his life. 'God wants to heal someone here tonight,' he told us, 'someone who is deaf.'

There were about two hundred and fifty people present. We were sitting at a table as far removed from the speaker's table as it was possible to be.

'Will all those who are deaf and wearing a hearing-aid please raise your hands?' he asked.

Several people responded, but I didn't move. I felt too proud to admit my problem in front of everybody. The speaker repeated his request. Peter kicked me discreetly under the table. It was as if everyone was waiting just for me. Slowly, I raised my hand, conscious of the surprised look on Lester and Julia's faces.

'Now, I'd like you to remove your hearing-aids and

place them on the table in front of you,' the speaker continued.

We all took them off and many put them on the table in their little black carrying-boxes.

'All hold hands,' he commanded, 'except the people on either side of those who are responding. I'd like you to place your hands over their ears.'

By this time I could hear nothing at all. I was too far away from the speaker to lip-read and, as my ears were covered, I experienced a marked increase in the volume of tinnitus, from which I also suffered. But I could still see, so I watched him begin to pray.

After a while, my attention began to wander and I thought I could hear a clock chiming the hour. This isn't a strange occurrence for a deaf person. High-frequency sounds often penetrate where other sounds can't. I glanced round the room looking for a clock, but couldn't find one.

Puzzled, I returned my attention to the speaker, only to realise that I could hear him speaking! Gradually the volume increased and I knew that in spite of all my doubts and embarrassment, even in spite of my pride, God had done it! He had heard the prayers of his people and restored my hearing.

Words can't express the excitement that followed. Peter says that I laughed and cried, shrieked and danced and covered my ears, all at the same time. I remember little about the detail, only the excitement – and the pain that was to follow when things sounded too loud. As we left the hotel I discovered that the clock I'd heard chiming the hour was in the main foyer. I'd heard it through two sets of swing-doors!

The next morning at four I woke to hear a loud rumbling sound. 'Peter, Peter, wake up,' I cried in terror. 'Wake up. We're having an earthquake!'

'It's all right,' he reassured me. 'It's only a freight train passing.'

I'd failed to identify a noise I'd never heard before,

in spite of the fact that it had occurred six nights out of seven since we'd moved into the house.

We had an out-of-service railway line beyond our back garden, used only by a local factory for transporting freight. I was familiar with the train going up and down the track during the day. But I'd never seen or heard the night trains.

During the next few weeks life became a catalogue of new experiences, not all of them pleasant. In each experience, however, God had something new to teach me.

Three weeks later, I had to take Joshua, our youngest son, for a routine visit to the family doctor.

'How are your ears these days, Mrs Beach?' she asked.

I was surprised. She hardly ever asked about them. Eagerly, I began to tell her that God had healed me. Knowing us well as a family and that we were Christians, she was only gently cynical.

'Perhaps we should arrange a visit to the consultant,' she suggested, thinking that he would soon sort out all this nonsense. But I welcomed the chance to show the consultant what God had done for me.

He wasn't as gentle in his scepticism. 'Go and have an audiology test now,' he ordered. So I went through to see the technician in her tiny office. She put the headphones on me and began the test.

We had a pantomime of false starts. Nobody had told her that I could hear now. Unable to believe the readings the machine was giving, she was convinced it was broken. Eventually, however, she sent me back to the consultant with the report that my hearing was 'within perfect limits'.

He was visibly shaken when he read it. I skipped back to the car, oblivious to the amused glances of passers-by, just delighted to have been discharged as a patient. Now I was secure in the knowledge that only Jesus could have caused those dead cells to live again and so restore my ability to hear.

Twelve years have passed since that day and my hearing is still excellent, more accurate even than Peter's! The tinnitus has never returned and, as a bonus, I'm now able to sing spontaneously.

I'd never been able to hear a tune correctly before, and could only sing at all as a result of the painstaking efforts of a dear friend who taught singing in schools. My repertoire was therefore decidedly limited. Now I've discovered that God has given me a singing voice with which to praise him whenever I choose. I regularly sing publicly in the meetings.

I've learnt many things through this experience – that we must allow God to be God, that pride is a sin, and that nothing compares with the love of God for his children.

But the greatest thing I learned was as a result of being deaf rather than being healed. Being deaf taught me to *listen*. And I hope I've carried this with me into the hearing world, to listen to others and to listen to God himself.

12

'I thought God was like Father Christmas'

Lila Feather, Haworth

I wasn't particularly keen on going to church with my friend, Patricia. I couldn't see the point in wasting time singing hymns and listening to a man droning on about God. It all seemed so out of touch with reality.

I grew up believing in God the same way I believed in Father Christmas. You ignored him all year round until you wanted something.

It was all a game, a trick to make you feel better when times were rough. I prayed when I needed help, like everyone does, but without believing that anything would really happen.

Remote, uncaring, maybe not even real. That was the hollow sham of a God I knew until Patricia persuaded me to go church with her.

'This is different, Lila,' she told me. 'You've never seen anything like this before.'

She was right! Even the building surprised me.

There were no hard wooden pews, stained-glass windows or spire. Instead, I found the church met above the local do-it-yourself store. It was a warm, welcoming place to walk into, tastefully decorated in soft shades of green and cream.

'The church isn't a building,' Patricia explained. 'The church is made up of *people*.'

There was no organ, but a lively band of guitars, drums and keyboard. No hushed voices and echoing, vaulted roof, but crowds of laughing, chattering people, excitedly greeting their friends. I was instantly made welcome.

I felt like a child looking wistfully in through a sweet-shop window. Life had been hard for me, and I felt so depressed. These folk seemed to have all the happiness and enthusiasm that I lacked. How I longed to be like them!

I was married young. We had four lovely children and lived on a farm on the edge of Haworth Moor in Yorkshire. It was bleak, wild country, stunningly beautiful in summer, harsh and cold in winter.

I'll never forget the day my husband went out into the fields and found his father lying dead on the ground. His grief was inconsolable. I tried to comfort him as best I could, but he suffered a complete nervous breakdown.

The next six years were a living hell. My husband changed completely as his moods dominated our lives. Bill, a friend of the family, was very supportive and I turned to him for comfort. He was so good and kind to me that eventually, even though he was married and we knew it was wrong, we fell in love.

I left the farm on the moors and moved, with my two youngest children, to a small cottage nearer the village. Bill continued to visit me there.

One day he called to see me and I knew something was very wrong. 'I've got cancer, Lila,' he said, 'lung cancer. The doctors say there's nothing they can do about it.'

I could hardly believe it!

'Will you pray for me?' he asked. 'I'm sure God'll heal me if we ask him.'

I didn't believe it, but I prayed anyway. Three months later, Bill died.

Depression hung around me like a cloak. I was ill myself, having just had a hysterectomy. Weak after my major operation, grieving for Bill, life felt really wretched.

Brenda, a young friend, called to see me regularly. 'Why don't you come to the Christian ladies' meeting in Haworth?' she asked me time and time again.

I didn't want to, and I put her off as often as I could. But eventually, just to keep her quiet, I agreed to go.

When I walked into the room I could see that these people had something special about them, something I wanted. Before I went home they prayed for God to strengthen me.

To my surprise, I felt much happier and stronger. 'Would you like to go with me next week, Jennifer?' I asked my daughter-in-law. She agreed, and we went together.

I watched as she prayed, asking Jesus to come into her life and make her a new person. She was absolutely radiant!

'If she can do it, so can I,' I determined, and I prayed, too. But unlike Jennifer I didn't feel any different at all.

The next Sunday, Patricia arrived in her car to take me to Airedale Church, Keighley. For the first time in my life I saw tangible evidence that God was real and that he cared for individuals. One after another had a story to tell of how God had answered their prayer. They seemed to know him as a friend, not as the remote stranger of my experience.

But somehow, as soon as I returned home, all the old worries and problems crowded in on me and life didn't seem any different. God was still far away. When I prayed, I couldn't pour out my love for him as other members of the church did. I just came with a list of things I wanted him to do for me.

As the weeks went by and my prayers never seemed to be answered, doubts crept in. 'Maybe I wasn't born again after all,' I sighed. 'God doesn't care for me in the same way as the others.'

It was with a terrible shock that I discovered I had a lump in my breast. I hurried round to see my doctor and he quickly arranged for me to go into hospital.

'I'm afraid we must operate in the morning,' the consultant told me. 'The lump may be benign, in other words, not harmful. But there's a chance that it may be malignant.'

Cancer!

'What can you do?' I asked fearfully.

'If the lump's benign we'll simply remove it,' he explained. 'But if it's cancerous we'll have to remove your breast, too.'

After he had gone, I lay in the hospital bed and prayed as I had never prayed before. I wasn't afraid of dying. But I was afraid for my son, Robert. He was only nineteen. Who would take care of *him* if anything happened me?

'Oh, God, help me,' I pleaded. 'I'm so frightened.' The words were barely out of my mouth when I heard footsteps.

It was a young nurse. She beamed a radiant smile at me and wandered casually round the room admiring all the cards and flowers the people from church had sent.

'Are you a born-again Christian?' she asked suddenly. 'I am.'

I could hardly believe it! I told her how I felt and that I had just prayed for God to help me.

She flung her arms around me and hugged me tight. 'It's going to be all right, Lila,' she said confidently. 'I'm going to pray for you now and ask God to fill you with his peace.'

That night, all anxiety gone, I slept like a baby.

I came round from my operation the next day to find the ward sister sitting beside my bed. 'I'm sorry, Lila, but the lump was cancerous,' she said gently. 'The surgeon had to remove your breast and the glands underneath your arm.'

'What happens now?' I asked, when her words had finally sunk in.

'We have no way of knowing if the cancer has spread to any other parts of your body,' she explained. 'We need to transfer you soon to the radiotherapy unit at Cookridge Hospital in Leeds.'

My heart sank. The thought of radiotherapy treatment terrified me. I would be treated twice every day for three weeks. Fear built up inside my mind, torturing me with thoughts of possible side-effects.

Then a letter arrived from one of the ladies in the church. 'Don't be afraid of the machines,' she wrote. 'Think of them as instruments that God will use to cure you. Spend the time you are under the machines praying. And while you're confined to bed in the hospital, read your Bible.'

So began an amazing three weeks of discovering God in a way I had never dreamed possible. The image of Father Christmas was shattered as I learned to know and love God as a friend. My list of wants vanished as my prayer times under the radiotherapy machines turned into intimate conversations. I went home a different person.

A year went by and I grew strong and well again. As I became a genuine part of the church, life took on a whole new dimension. I was no longer on the outside looking in, but fully involved and able to say confidently that God's love for me was real.

At the end of the year I found another lump. Memories of the last painful experience flooded back as I faced the possibility of another operation.

Surely I wasn't going to have to go through all that again? I knew that the doctors who'd operated on me previously had saved my life. I had met only kindness and understanding from all the hospital staff, and I was grateful for their skill and expertise. But the thought of suffering the pain and trauma of another mastectomy was just dreadful.

I told the church what had happened and they gathered round, laid their hands on me and prayed. We prayed, not like children bringing their lists to Father Christmas, but confidently. I was certain that the God who loved and cared for me personally would do whatever was best for me.

My doctor rushed me into hospital. But this time, as I lay waiting to go down to theatre, I felt no fear at all, just peace and confidence that God was taking care of me.

When I came round from the anaesthetic a somewhat puzzled ward sister was there.

'Was it cancer?' I asked sleepily.

'Lila, it's gone!' she exclaimed. 'The surgeon couldn't find a lump at all!'

How can cancer, the most feared of all diseases, just go away? Yet the lump has gone and three years later still hasn't come back. Only God can work such a miracle.

The memory of the young nurse who came to comfort me when I was so ill and frightened, remains vividly with me. So I regularly visit the local Sue Ryder Hospice to sit with dying patients. I comfort them, pray for them and, where possible, introduce them to my best friend, Jesus.

13

'God really does give us abundant life!'

Monika Hall, Bath

In October 1985 I faced a really exciting challenge. After ten years at home bringing up our four children, I was about to return to the classroom and begin part-time teaching.

The first day went well. I enjoyed myself, discovering some of the changes that had overtaken school during my long absence from teaching.

At home I cooked the evening meal, spent time with the children and planned the next day's lessons. I went to bed that night feeling a real sense of achievement.

I woke in the early hours of the morning with a severe headache. That's unusual for me. I'm not a headachy sort of person. I just took two paracetamol and put it down to excitement – and, of course, stress. People had kept telling me how stressful teaching had become!

By morning I was considerably worse, so much so

that my husband wanted to call the doctor.

'No, don't bother, Derek,' I protested. 'I've probably got flu. The doctor couldn't do anything about that.'

Reluctantly, he agreed.

Throughout the day, as friends called in to see me, they did their best to persuade me to call the doctor.

'No, no,' I insisted. 'I'm sure it'll go away soon.' But despite my optimism I got worse, not better.

The next day and a half were a strange mixture of searing pain and a feeling of being disembodied, somehow uninvolved in what was happening. Yet still I clung to my unshakeable conviction that we'd look really silly making a fuss about a simple dose of flu.

The following morning, Derek was so worried that he phoned our doctor and asked him to visit me. By this time I was in no fit state to protest.

Our doctor arrived after some considerable delay, took one look round the bedroom door and immediately went to phone for an ambulance.

Of the next two days in hospital I remember practically nothing. But my husband has filled me in on some of the highlights.

As the ambulance drove away, lights flashing, Derek leapt into his car to follow in procession. But halfway there the car broke down. The ambulance disappeared into the distance leaving Derek stranded at the roadside. Abandoning the car, he set off to find a taxi. And, having tracked one down, he sped across the city in hot pursuit.

Things weren't too good when he arrived at the hospital. My dose of flu actually turned out to be meningitis. The course of action was twofold: first, to establish whether it was viral or bacterial meningitis; and second, to bring down my temperature, which had reached a hundred and five degrees!

'Do you mean to tell me that your wife's temperature has been soaring unchecked for *two days?'* asked the consultant in surprise.

'Well, we've never had a thermometer,' admitted Derek. 'We had no way of knowing how hot was hot.'

The consultant wasn't impressed.

Early evening came and things were, if anything, worse than when I was admitted. No amount of ice or cold fans in the room did anything to help.

The consultant came and took my husband quietly to one side. 'If her temperature doesn't drop within a very short time, I'm afraid the outlook could be grim,' he said solemnly. 'I think you'd better remain close by.'

As the full implications of the consultant's words hit him, Derek's strength and optimism faded slightly. It was imperative that my runaway temperature be brought under control, otherwise my chances of survival were slim.

Quickly he phoned the elders of our church and explained the situation to them. The church folk were gathering together that evening for a prayer meeting. As Derek sat praying beside my bed, he knew that many others were supporting him with *their* prayers, too.

Quite suddenly, with no warning at all, my temperature plummeted to below normal. And it stayed there, steady as a rock.

Afterwards we discovered that this was the exact moment when the church switched from praying for my healing to thanking God in faith for what he had already done.

I left the hospital soon after that with many warnings ringing in my ears about the repercussions of such a severe attack.

'You'll feel very weak for a long time,' the staff told me helpfully.

Our children were delighted to have me home again but furious that I'd made my dramatic departure when they were at school. They'd missed it all!

'If you've got to go again, wait till we get home,' they demanded.

I actually recovered very quickly indeed. Within a year I was back into teaching full-time. Now, five years on, I'm fit, healthy and energetic. I work as head of faculty in a large boys' school in Avon. I take a full part in all the school's activities, including the health and fitness programme.

Derek works within the teaching profession, too. He is deputy headteacher of a large school. They're both demanding jobs that require a lot of stamina.

We spend our leisure time gardening, doing up our large house, playing squash and caring for a homegroup in our church. It's great. God really does give us an abundant life!

God's faithfulness to us left an impression that will never fade. We feel totally confident of his love and protection. Although in some ways it was a very frightening experience, in others it was an exciting one. We both knew the awesome presence of our God, even in the face of death itself.

Derek and I appreciate each other and our lives together much more now. There's nothing like almost losing something to make you enjoy it all the more.

14

'I had to remember to trust God'

Vera Peek, Weston-super-Mare

There was no apparent reason for the pain in my hips and legs. I just woke up one morning and there it was, a stiff, nagging sort of pain which made walking a misery and my housework difficult.

I hate taking tablets of any kind, but as the pain was so intense, I took some paracetamol and hoped it would soon wear off. But it didn't. Week after week went by, yet I didn't feel any better at all.

'If this doesn't clear up soon I'm going to have to see the doctor,' I thought each day. But I'm a busy woman and very active, even though I'm retired and a grandma, too. I kept putting off making an appointment, having neither the time nor the inclination to be ill.

The crunch came when I got up one morning to find the pain had increased drastically. I tried to get out of bed. But as I got to my feet I collapsed in agony.

Reg, my husband, was at my side immediately.

'This has gone on long enough,' he decided. 'I'm calling the doctor now.'

My own family doctor was away on a study course. His locum, a tall, lanky young Irishman, arrived quickly.

'I think perhaps you have an infection in your bladder,' he said after he'd finished examining me. 'That would account for the pain and stiffness in your hips.'

He took away a sample of my urine to test and left me a prescription for some antibiotics. I stayed in bed, hoping to be better within a few days.

But the problem wasn't a bladder infection at all. When, after completing the five-day antibiotic course, I was still in great pain, he arranged for me to visit the local hospital for some tests.

We've got a smart new hospital in Weston now. But eleven years ago, at the time I went along for all those tests, out-patients' was held in an old Victorian building on the seafront.

It was absolutely freezing. I sat in my flimsy hospital gown with my teeth chattering as the draughts blasted down the corridors and swirled under the cubicle door.

The X-ray department was on the other side of town at another building, equally old and draughty. Reg drove me there a few days later and I had to undergo the unpleasant experience of a barium meal.

I sat in the doctor's surgery and waited expectantly for the results of all the tests I'd undergone.

'I'm sorry, Mrs Peek, but I'm afraid it isn't good news,' he said. 'I have to tell you that you have osteoarthrosis of your lower pelvis.'

'Will it get better?' I asked, horrified at the prospect of having to suffer so much pain indefinitely.

'I'm afraid not,' he answered. 'We can only help to control the pain.'

He went on to explain that the damage had actually been done many years ago, when I was giving birth to my son.

I'd suffered a lot with back pain during my pregnancy. I'm a small woman and I'd had a large, healthy baby. But the strain had obviously been too much. My back had suffered permanent damage. Why, after all these years of lying dormant, the trouble should suddenly flare up so violently, no-one could explain.

I left the surgery with a prescription for some enormous orange tablets. They certainly eased the pain, but I hated taking them and managed with as few as possible.

I found the work of running our big old house almost impossible now. But the more my joints seized up with stiffness, the more determined I became to overcome my disability.

'I *will* keep walking,' I wept, frustrated that I couldn't even struggle to the end of the garden path.

'Vera, go and sit down,' Reg insisted. 'You really need to rest.'

We had booked a caravan holiday at Blaithwaite Camp, near Keswick in Cumbria. I was struggling so much with the pain in my back and legs that caravanning didn't really appeal to me.

But Blaithwaite was no ordinary camp. It was a nationwide gathering of Christians. We came together for worship and teaching and just to enjoy each other's company.

I knew that great emphasis was always placed on God's power to heal the sick. So, faint-hearted as I felt at the thought of roughing it for a week, wild horses wouldn't have kept me away.

Reg and I are committed Christians. We've often seen people healed through prayer. We were certain that I would leave that camp whole and well again.

We drove slowly north, taking two days to make the journey to allow me time to rest between each stage. Our ten-year-old granddaughter, Rachel, came with us.

The weather wasn't kind to us. It poured with rain all week. Campers trudged about in their wellies, the field around the meeting-tent becoming a sea of mud.

In the cold damp conditions, the pain in my hips and legs was absolutely excruciating. But despite my discomfort, I struggled along to every meeting. Although I was prayed for, to my surprise I felt no better.

On the last night of the camp, five thousand people gathered together to break bread and share wine. It was a wonderful celebration of God's goodness to us. But tears of disappointment trickled down my cheeks. I'd been so sure that God would heal me. Now the week was gone and I would return home still in pain.

Then one of the leaders, John Hutchison, came to the microphone to speak.

'There are ten people here crying out for healing,' he said. 'Come out to the front of the meeting and we'll pray for you.'

Hope rose once more. Reg and Rachel helped me to the front. By now I was so stiff with pain and cold it was difficult to walk unaided.

As John laid his hands on my shoulders and began to pray, a terrific warmth spread through my body. The cold receded, and with it the pain.

A great peace flowed through me and I began to laugh and laugh. Tears of joy now poured down my face. I went back to my seat, thrilled at what God had done.

The next morning the first thing I noticed when I woke up was that the pain had gone, completely gone! After many weeks of misery, the relief was tremendous.

I jumped out of bed, delighted to feel well enough to help Reg with the packing. I still had a bit of a limp in my right leg but I didn't care. At least the pain was gone.

But delighted as I was to be free from all pain,

dragging along a stiff leg is no joke. When we got home I felt clumsy and awkward. Reg and I love walking, but I couldn't go far at all without my leg suddenly collapsing beneath me. It was so frustrating.

True, I hadn't needed any painkillers since John had prayed for me. But with my leg so stiff I didn't know whether or not the pain would come back. So I kept a few painkillers in my handbag, just in case I should need them.

I'm grateful that I had a good next-door neighbour at that time. Twice a week Madge arrived to help me clean and to push the Hoover round. I don't know how I'd have managed without her support. Apart from the practical help she gave, she and others from our church prayed regularly for me.

When autumn came, we went to Exmouth for a week, to a conference at Haldon Court. We were pleased to see that John Hutchison was the speaker again.

I loved to listen to that man. As we sat down expectantly in the meeting, I felt confident that he would have something good to say.

John immediately launched into a familiar Bible story. I knew it well. Peter, in his boat with the other disciples on the sea of Galilee, sees Jesus walking on the water towards him.

'Come,' said Jesus, holding out his hands. And Peter leapt out of the boat and actually began to walk on the water. Suddenly, he took his eyes off Jesus and, seeing the size of the waves and the strength of the storm around him, began to sink.

'Peter started well,' explained John. 'He *did* walk on the water. But as soon as he took his eyes off Jesus and looked at his circumstances, he began to sink.

'We're like that sometimes,' he continued. 'We start out well. But when our difficulties threaten to overwhelm us, if we take our eyes off Jesus we're sunk!'

A vision of a large orange tablet swam before my eyes. I ignored it, trying to concentrate on what John was saying. Persistently, it filled my thoughts until, with a terrible shock, I realised what God was saying to me.

I, too, was guilty of unbelief. I started out well, just like Peter. When I had become ill I was full of faith and God had healed me. But when the difficulties came, when the limp wouldn't go and my leg kept collapsing, I put my faith in a bottle of orange tablets. God said I was healed. But I had hung on to them, just in case the pain came back.

Leaving my seat, I crept out of the meeting hall and into the ladies' toilet. I opened my handbag, took out the tablets I always kept there and flushed them down the toilet. Then I made my way quietly back to my seat.

As soon as I sat down, I felt strength flow into my right leg. It was quite unmistakable. The difference was amazing.

That afternoon, Reg and I went for the first good walk we'd had in months. We tramped for three miles across the sandy beach. I suffered no pain or ill effects at all. I learned a valuable lesson that day and, eleven years on, I'm still living in the good of it.

15

'It's great to feel well!'

Hendrika Andrews, South Molton

I've been ill almost all my life. So you can imagine how thrilled I am to be healed.

'How are things with you these days, Hendrika?' my friends ask when I meet them.

'It's like living in paradise,' I reply. 'Life's wonderful, and feeling well is great!' After years of heart trouble, at last I can honestly say that I'm fitter than many other people my age.

I first became ill when I was only seven years old. I developed rheumatic fever, a serious illness sixty years ago, which left me with a damaged heart valve.

Despite that setback, I grew up reasonably well and strong, and as soon as I was old enough I started training to be a nurse.

It was hard work but I was coping well. Then, when I was in the third year of my training, I picked up an infection.

I developed endomyocarditis. This inflammation

of the heart left me in such a weakened state that my nursing career was ended. Sadly, I left the hospital. At the age of twenty-two I was pronounced a semi-invalid.

Holland, my native country, has such low-lying land that the atmosphere there is heavy. Even though my parents were farmers and lived out in the country, I was constantly weak and found it difficult to breathe.

'The best thing for you is to move to another country,' the doctors advised me. 'You need somewhere mild but fresh.'

I moved to England in 1947 and made my home in South Molton, a lovely part of Devon. Slowly, I grew stronger. I was never able to live a full and active life like other people but I got out and about as much as I could. I've always hated being ill and fought hard against it.

I'm a Christian and have a deep, strong faith in God. I believed he wanted me well and I never stopped praying, asking him to heal me. But alongside that, I accepted that doctors had a lot to offer. Their expertise and medication saved my life on more than one occasion, and I'm very grateful to them for their help. But I wanted to be well.

I married a lovely Englishman, Frederick, and although we never had any children we had many happy years together. While we were on holiday together in Germany, I suffered a heart attack.

All the strength I'd built up so painstakingly over the years was gone, lost in a moment of terrifying illness. When I recovered enough to return home to Devon I started again, praying for health and strength. I just longed to live a normal life.

Healing Meeting. I looked at the poster advertising the meeting to be held at a local church. I was willing to try anything, so we went along, hoping for a miracle.

'Will all those wanting prayer come out to the

front?' the speaker announced. I walked out to the front of the hall with all the other sick people. So many sick, tired people, all hoping that this man's prayer would change their lives.

But nothing happened for me. That was the first of many times when I visited churches and meetings. In my quest for health I heard a lot of speakers, had plenty of prayers spoken over me, but nothing ever changed. I remained as weak and ill as before.

Nine years went by and I continued to see the specialist at the hospital. He was always very kind and reassuring, but we both knew that he could do nothing to cure my condition. At best, he could only help me to control it.

Another bout of myocarditis set me back considerably. And a third attack weakened me even further. How I longed to be free of all this illness! I fought my way back as hard as I could. Whenever I heard of a church holding a healing meeting, I would go if I possibly could. But each time I went I was disappointed.

The news that my father had died suddenly came as a terrible shock to me. It was the beginning of the most traumatic time of my life.

Four days later, while I was still reeling from the shock of his death, my husband also died, of cancer. This was followed ten weeks later by the death of my mother. Unable to accept the loss of her husband, she died broken-hearted, overcome with grief.

Words cannot describe the desolation I felt at my triple bereavement. Anyone who has ever lost someone they loved dearly will understand. But to lose three, so close together, was a terrible experience.

My heart, already in a weakened state, suffered badly from the effect of my grief and within six months I was dangerously ill.

Like a broken watch-spring, my heart now went completely out of control. Faster and faster it beat, pumping the blood so quickly that it couldn't get out of my heart chamber fast enough.

My heart valve, damaged when I had rheumatic fever as a child, started leaking under the excess pressure. Blood, leaking back into the chamber instead of flowing out, formed a clot.

The hospital specialist prescribed Verapamil, 40mg a day. But it had no effect. He upped the dose, first to 80mg, then to 120mg, still with no effect. Finally, in desperation, he doubled the dose yet again to 240mg, but still my heart wouldn't slow down. Like a runaway horse, it continued its galloping course.

Ill and bereaved, I needed to find a place where I could meet with people who could support me at such a time.

'I wonder about that church in Barnstaple,' I thought. 'It's not like any other church I've been to.'

I was frankly curious about these people. Everyone knew that there was something special about them. I wanted to find out what exactly they believed and how their faith in God affected their lives.

The meeting was held at the Queen's Hall in the town centre. I was really fascinated by everyone's enthusiasm and spontaneity of worship. When the speaker, Raymond Manoehoetoe, asked if anyone wanted prayer for healing, I was taken by surprise. I'd been so busy thinking about the worship we were enjoying that I'd forgotten about being ill!

Raymond laid his hands on me and began to pray. And incredibly, wonderfully, my runaway heart came right back under control and began beating normally.

God is so full of surprises! All those years I'd trailed from one healing meeting to another with no success. And now, when healing was far from my mind, when I was just enjoying worshipping him, he stepped in and healed me.

It wasn't a gradual change at all. One moment I was ill, the next, gloriously healed.

The specialist, when I saw him two months later, was amazed to see me looking so well.

'What about the drugs I prescribed you?' he asked. 'You *are* taking those – aren't you?'

'Well, no,' I admitted. 'I don't need them anymore.'

He gave me a thorough examination and confirmed that my heart was better. 'I'll be writing to your family doctor,' he said.

A few days before Christmas, I walked briskly along to my doctor's surgery, I who had previously had to creep along at a snail's pace.

As I walked into his surgery he greeted me with a joyful smile.

'You've won, you've won, you've won, Rika,' he declared excitedly.

'What do you mean?' I asked.

Waving a piece of paper about, he explained, 'I've received a delightful letter from the specialist.'

'That Dutch lady of yours has beaten her heart condition,' he read. 'I hope to see her again in two years' time.'

I was excited, too, of course, as I told him about the healing meeting. 'My heart slowed down to normal the moment Raymond prayed for me,' I said. 'What's more, it's stayed normal ever since!'

'I'm delighted to hear that, Rika,' he said warmly. 'I wish you well. Now keep well, and come to see me again in six months' time.'

More than two years have gone by since my healing. Today I'm a fit person. I don't need any drugs at all, thanks to God's healing power and grace through the prayers of faithful believers.

16

'Prayer works – God is faithful to his word'

Ian Critchley, Wakefield

How can I begin to describe the love, faithfulness and support our family experienced during a major crisis in April 1990?

I'm the pastor of the City Church in Wakefield, West Yorkshire. They're a lovely group of people – enthusiastic, warm and caring. When tragedy struck, they rallied round immediately.

The day began like any other Sunday, with a meeting of the church at the Unity Hall in Wakefield. The children were meeting in a separate room, having an action-packed session of games, singing and teaching.

They were playing a running-around game, letting off steam before sitting down to listen to their teacher. Our three children, Wesley, aged nine, Hannah, eight, and Matthew, five, were in there thoroughly enjoying themselves.

Suddenly, a very large free-standing coatstand

overbalanced. Before anyone could catch it, the stand crashed down on top of Matthew. A large hook pierced his skull, penetrating his brain just above and behind his right ear. He screamed in agony.

Stuart Reece, an Australian surgeon working locally at Pinderfields Hospital, was in our meeting that morning. He and another member of the church, staff nurse Ruth Cox, carefully eased the hook from Matthew's head and freed him from the coatstand.

We picked him up and carried him to the car. My wife, Rachel, along with Stuart and Ruth, all accompanied us to the hospital. We raced across the city, praying continually for our little boy's life.

As soon as we arrived at the accident and emergency department, Stuart sprang into action. He handed Matthew over to the staff on duty. He then ordered an immediate brain scan and an anaesthetist and operating theatre to be standing by. Within forty-five minutes Matthew was undergoing major surgery.

We waited outside for the longest hour and a half of our lives until, finally, the neurosurgeon emerged.

'Well,' he began, 'I'm afraid you have a brain-damaged son.'

The shock of his words was like a physical blow.

'A part of Matthew's brain, about the size of a squashed golf-ball, has been destroyed,' the surgeon went on. 'We had to remove many other bits of fragmented brain, too.'

'How bad is the damage?' I asked. 'What effect will it have?'

'There's a significant chance that he'll be epileptic,' the surgeon replied. 'Apart from that you'll just have to wait and see what other abnormalities develop.'

He went on to explain the various complications and problems that could occur. They might include mental and personality problems, fits, black-outs – in fact, a whole catalogue of brain-related disorders.

'They could arise at any time during the next two

years,' he said. 'But if he makes it through the next couple of years without anything serious developing, his chances increase.'

I knew that the surgeon who had performed such a delicate operation on our little son was an extremely skilled man, and I felt grateful to him for all he had done. But I also knew that his skill was limited. The gloomy prognosis he offered was based on his experience of such cases. He had done his best. Matthew would probably survive, but he would never be the same lively, mischievous little boy we had loved.

As the surgeon told me these things, faith inside my heart refused to accept them. It wasn't stubbornness or an unwillingness to face facts. I confronted them honestly. But at the same time I knew that the best the surgeon had to offer wasn't good enough.

I also knew that God could do better. I was certain that it was not God's will for Matthew to suffer permanent brain damage.

Rachel agreed. 'I'm sure God won't just bring him through this accident,' she said. 'I know he'll recreate the damaged brain so that Matthew can live an absolutely normal life and fulfil the purpose God has for him.'

Matthew was such a brave little boy. He came through the operation very well. One-half of his head had been shaved of hair and he had an enormous scar running from behind his ear to the top of his head.

As I sat with Rachel, praying beside Matthew's bed, it seemed as if the whole world was praying with us. Our church has learnt to pray effectively and they got straight into action as soon as the full extent of Matthew's injury was realised.

All nine of our regional homegroups met to pray for Matthew's full recovery. Some people stayed up all night, others fasted as they prayed.

Churches across the UK joined us. The word even spread to the USA and South Africa. People there –

some who knew us, others who didn't – joined together to call on God for a full restoration of Matthew's brain.

'We'll call him "Wholeson",' we decided, 'because it's God will for him to be whole again.'

Within two days Matthew was much brighter. He sat up in bed sporting a neat pair of 'Dennis the Menace' pyjamas. We were glad to see him looking so much better. But we were careful to look to *God* for our encouragement, not to the circumstantial signs on our son's face.

'When will Matthew be able to go home?' asked Rachel on Tuesday, when the surgeon made his ward round.

'Not for another two weeks,' he replied cautiously.

But Matthew was recovering by leaps and bounds. He improved so much overnight that the surgeon reconsidered.

'If he continues to progress at this rate we may be able to send him home in time for Easter,' he decided.

Easter! But that was only a few days away. Matthew's accident had happened on Sunday 8 April. Easter Sunday was on the fifteenth, only a week later.

Then, on Thursday 12 April, just four days after major surgery, Matthew was well enough to be discharged. The staff examined his wound and declared it so well healed that the fourteen stitches could come out. 'You can take him home today,' they announced.

We were thrilled.

You would have to have seen the brain scan or understood the extent of his injuries to know just what a major miracle this was. Our God has done great things.

Once back home, Matthew progressed in a remarkable way. He is a completely normal child. None of the abnormalities or problems the surgeon predicted have manifested themselves. He has no mental problems, no blackouts, no epilepsy.

After coming home he was tired and, as his body recovered from the shock, he needed extra rest times during the afternoon. But otherwise he's been completely well.

In June, Matthew was ready to go back school. Rachel took him along, only to find that the school didn't feel able to accept responsibility for him.

'But he's perfectly well and back to normal,' Rachel insisted.

The headteacher wasn't so sure. 'He might bang his head again,' she said. 'I'm sorry, but I can't take the risk.'

Officially, Matthew suffered brain damage from his accident. The headmistress, having only the official hospital report to go on, felt he should be cared for in a special school.

It was obvious we would have a little persuading to do. An appointment was made for us to see the education department's own doctor.

'Well, I can find no evidence of any abnormality at all,' she declared. She recommended that Matthew be allowed back to school.

Another appointment followed, this time with the senior neurosurgeon at Pinderfields Hospital.

'Matthew isn't showing any sign of abnormality,' he said, 'so you're free to go. I don't need to see him again unless there are any problems.'

'Bye-bye, doctor,' we shouted as we drove away from the hospital. 'We won't be seeing you again!'

We knew all along that God had healed Matthew, but it was wonderful to have it confirmed again and again.

At last Matthew could go back to school, but with one compromise. We accepted that he should come home for lunch every day. It seemed fair enough. The sort of antics five-year-old boys get up to are enough to stop the heart of even the bravest dinner lady, without having to keep a special eye on one child in particular.

We really praise God for the miracle he performed. We have a 'Wholeson'. God did it for us. This is a tremendous illustration of thousands of Christians joining their hearts and faith together to pray.

'I can't ever remember witnessing such a ready response of so many people in so many countries to pray over one little boy,' declare the pastors of several churches.

Neither can I. But when we joined our faith together, God answered.

Afterword

Peter Reynolds

You, too, can claim a miracle. Miracles *do* happen! They're happening to ordinary people from all walks of life in your area.

This isn't a local phenomenon. The testimonies in this book are told by people who live throughout the length and breadth of the UK. It's not the work of one man with a particular gift of faith for healing. Neither is it solely the result of church leaders praying for their own congregation.

It's encouraging to see that anyone, even a new Christian, can pray for a miracle and see God at work. God is doing grass roots work among his people. A greater level of faith and expectancy has risen over the years, with corresponding results. And the old 'if it be thy will' escape clause has largely disappeared from our prayers.

Of course, we have a great deal more to learn about praying for the sick. But we have every reason to be encouraged. And if you or someone you love is ill, begin crying out to God. You, too, can claim the miracle of healing.

Natural and supernatural conditions

We know that it is God's will that 'you may enjoy good health and that all may go well with you, even as your soul is getting along well'.[1] So we are certain that sickness is an enemy and never sent by God for any reason.

Remember also that your health will get along well 'even as your soul is getting along well'. Spiritual and emotional well-being are inextricably linked with physical health. Bitterness, resentment and anxiety often go hand in hand with sickness. This isn't a punishment from God, simply a natural consequence of living with a wrong attitude.

Many sicknesses have a natural remedy. If you get a bad cough or cold following many nights of very little sleep – at a time when your body is tired and run down – it's probably not prayer you need. You just need to apply a little commonsense wisdom. A good night's sleep can work wonders in giving your physical mechanism the chance it needs to restore you to normal health.

On the other hand, we mustn't forget that there is a spiritual war going on. Spiritual forces are actively opposed to your well-being. Demons are set to bring destruction. Meanwhile, the Holy Spirit is constantly ready to heal and restore.

Don't ignore this fact. Spiritual forces need to be confronted by the Word of God in the Bible, and by the power of the Holy Spirit actively working within that Word to bring health and wholeness, healing and well-being.

'Nothing happened'

What happens when symptoms don't go away? 'I believed with all my heart,' we cry. 'I was prayed for and nothing happened. What about me?'

Prophesy to your own body. Lay hands on yourself and take authority through the Word and promises of God. This isn't cranky stuff. King David in the Bible spoke to himself. He asked his own soul some questions. Then he gave some commands to his own soul that he expected and required to be obeyed.[2]

This isn't mind over matter. It is simply making war, bringing about God's kingdom and rule through the promises and the Word he has already spoken.

When you speak and command with the Word of God, you are being a prophetic person. You are demonstrating that you are one who lives by what you have seen of God's will. You are saying, 'God's will be done on earth as it is in heaven.'

The symptoms have returned

What happens when symptoms come back? Expect them to go again. Require them to go. Demand that they go!

Paul writes, 'If the Spirit of him who raised Jesus from the dead is living in you, he who raised Christ from the dead will also give life to your mortal bodies through his Spirit, who lives in you.'[3]

The Greek word used here for 'give life', *zoopoieo*, says it all. Expect God to *zoopoieo* you! Expect the supernatural power of God to work in you.

'Those who hope in the Lord will renew their strength. They will soar on wings like eagles.'[4]

The word 'hope' here is taken from the Hebrew word *qavah*. *Qavah* means more than just wishful thinking. It means 'to expect' or 'to look for'. Therefore, expect and look for the supernatural *zoopoieo* of God, no matter how long you've had the condition or how bleak the medical prognosis.

The grave could not hold down Jesus when confronted by the power of God's Holy Spirit. Why should your physical condition be any different?

Those who trust in the Lord will not be

disappointed. You may get some setbacks, but you will not be disappointed. God will not disappoint those who trust him and expect him to act.

The shame of continued sickness

'If God wants everyone to live in health, sickness is a contradiction of the will of God.'

'If I am sick, I'm not living in the will of God, am I?'

'How do I cope with the disgrace of continued symptoms?'

Many people struggle with feelings of shame and guilt that they are still not physically whole, even after repeated prayer. 'How can I be prayed for yet again?' they wonder.

Take heart! If you are still sick, you're not a total failure. You are in the distinguished company of some of Paul's apostolic team who were troubled with ongoing physical sicknesses.

Jesus said that when we visit somebody who is sick we are doing it for him.[5] There may be a number of reasons why somebody is still sick after prayer. It doesn't necessarily mean that it's the sick person's fault any more than it is the fault of those who should be bringing healing to them.

Remember, one battle is not the whole war. Even if one or two battles go against you, you can still go on to win the war. Just because your enemy holds on to a patch of ground, or even temporarily regains some ground, that in itself doesn't indicate the outcome of the rest of the war. Never give up. With Jesus you *will* win!

What about doctors and medicines?

'Is it wrong to go to the doctor or into hospital?'

'Is it right or wrong to take medicine?'

'Doesn't the taking of medicine indicate that you don't really trust Jesus for your health and healing?'

Use every weapon at your disposal, including the help of doctors, medicines and hospitals, in your fight against disease and sickness. There is nothing wrong with using the knowledge and skill of doctors and the help of medicines.

There is, however, a whole lot of difference between trusting in Jesus for everything and transferring your trust to doctors and medicines. If you place your trust in hospitals, doctors and medicines you also confine yourself to their limited powers.

The power of God knows no such limitations.

If you place your trust only in the wisdom of medics, however skilled they may be, you restrict your physical well-being and your destiny to the limitations of their (albeit rapidly advancing) knowledge.

In that event, when a doctor tells you that you have not really been healed, even though the symptoms left your body immediately following prayer, you will tend to believe him rather than the power of God. You will expect your symptoms to return sooner or later because you believe you are only in remission. There is a strong likelihood, in that case, that they *will* return. You'll get what you have faith for!

Don't pull doctors down in your estimation and conversation in an attempt to show God's power in an even greater contrasting light. God doesn't need this. It would show a lack of integrity on your part and therefore is ungodly.

Doctors are highly-skilled people with valuable advice and help to offer. They are not to be avoided as our enemies. They are constantly saving lives and helping people to recovery through the use of their knowledge. They do an excellent job at what they can do.

In matters of faith, however, there are times when a choice has to be made: believe what the doctor says, or what God's Word says. There are occasions when it becomes necessary to lay aside the advice the doctor gives. You should do this only after careful consideration when you are sure that this is what God has told you to do.

Supposing, for instance, you decide to cease or refuse some medical treatment. You would be wise to consider the possible consequences carefully. If others, such as a husband, wife or children, could be affected by your decision, it would be honourable to discuss the situation with them first before taking any action.

When God heals you of something medically incurable, don't be too upset if your doctor doesn't accept that a notable miracle has taken place. If he is not a man of faith he may say you have merely had some sort of remission. Technically, as far as he is concerned, you still have the disease. He is simply saying that his scientific mind can't accept yet that you are, in clinical terms, cured.

Remember, he is not the ultimate and final authority on the matter. If you were sick and now you are well, you can still give thanks to God and tell others about it as an accomplished fact, in spite of the doctor's caution.

A faith to live by

It's a wonderful thing when you are released from a condition that you have struggled with for years. You find an empathy with the crippled man Jesus healed, who leapt around the place with sheer delight.[6] Particularly if you have been in pain for many years and you are healed, you have no difficulty from that point on in finding something to praise and thank God for.

As this book shows, there is a power far greater than the best of all the medical knowledge, skill and wisdom that there is in the whole world. This book has recounted just a few of the countless true stories throughout the UK and in every other country of the world. It tells of the power of God's Holy Spirit to do what medical science alone could never do.

Don't limit yourself to man's best. God can do far more than that. He showed this most graphically and powerfully when he raised Jesus bodily out of the grave and fully back to life after three whole days.

If he can do *that*, he can heal your cancer, remove your stomach ulcer or bring an end to your migraine headaches.

Remember the *zoopoieo* of God, found in Jesus Christ, his Son. Health and wholeness are yours by right when you put your trust in him. So go out and boldly claim your miracle!

NOTES

1. 3 John 2
2. See Psalm 42:5
3. Romans 8:11
4. Isaiah 40:31
5. Matthew 25:39–40
6. Acts 3:1–10